POLITICAL PORTRAITS

GENERAL EDITOR
KENNETH O. MORGAN

WILLIAM EWART GLADSTONE

AGATHA RAMM

GPC Books is an imprint of the University of Wales Press, 6 Gwennyth Street, Cardiff,
CF2 4YD

First published in 1989

© Agatha Ramm, 1989

British Library Cataloguing in Publication Data
Ramm, Agatha
William Ewart Gladstone. – (Political Portraits)
1. Great Britain. Gladstone, W.E. (William Ewart), 1809–1898
I. Title   II. Series
941.081'092'4
ISBN 0-7083-1044-3
ISBN 0-7083-1045-1 Pbk

Cover design: T.C. Evans, Logic Graphics

The publishers wish to acknowledge the advice and assistance given by the Design
Department of the Welsh Books Council which is supported by the Welsh Arts Council.

Set by Quality Phototypesetting Ltd., Bristol
Printed in Great Britain at The Bath Press, Avon

Contents

Editor's Foreword

The aim of this open-ended series of short biographies is to offer personal portraits of the decisive figures in the making of British politics over the past two hundred years. It will range over leading practitioners of politics, from Britain and Ireland (and probably the commonwealth/ empire as well) who have vitally shaped our public affairs in the nineteenth and twentieth centuries. Its premise, of course, is that people and biographies are vitally important as explanatory keys to the past. Too often, historians tend to see the course of historical change in terms of vague impersonal factors, evolutionary patterns, underlying themes, even that Scylla and Charybdis of historical understanding, 'forces' and 'trends'. The impact of the disciplines of economics, sociology or anthropology is often taken as reinforcing this tendency, and helping to obliterate flesh-and-blood human beings from our map of the past.

Now, no-one would seriously dispute the enrichment of historical studies that has resulted from the stimulus of other disciplines. At the same time, it can hardly be questioned that the role of key individuals, locally and regionally as well as nationally, has been crucial in shaping the rhythms and speed of our political development in the years since the twin impact of industrialization and representative democracy. The growth of our political parties are impossible to visualize without the personal imprint of Gladstone, Disraeli or Keir Hardie. The course of wars, and their consequences, would have been totally different if Lloyd George or Churchill had never lived. Without Parnell or de Valera, modern Ireland would not have emerged in its present form. Even in the 1980s, the dominance of Mrs Thatcher confirms anew the powerful impulses that can be released by the authority or whim of one determined individual.

So there need be no apology for offering a new series of biographies, brief but authoritative, all written by expert scholars, designed for the intelligent general reader as well as for the student or the specialist, as launch-pads for political and historical understanding. Portraits of individuals, naturally, open up wider social, cultural or intellectual themes. They also help to make history fun—vibrant, vivid, accessible. They may also be a means to a deeper understanding of our world. It should always be remembered that Karl Marx himself, whose influence is so frequently taken as eliminating individuals entirely from history in favour of the rise and conflict of social classes, actually took the reverse view himself. 'History', Marx wrote, 'is nothing but the activity of men in pursuit of their ends.' Some of these men—and women—and the ends they pursued, achieved, missed out on, or simply forgot, are illustrated in this series.

The dominating figure of Gladstone, that Victorian colossus, is examined in this book by Dr Agatha Ramm, a major authority on both British and European nineteenth-century history. Even after the publication of the superb edition of most of his diary by Dr H.C.G. Matthew, the 'G.O.M.' remains a peculiarly baffling and inaccessible personality. In character and outlook he was tempestuous and volcanic, powerfully intellectual but also a man of strong, barely controlled private emotions. In his long political career, he achieved a unique personal dominance as the concept 'Gladstonian Liberalism' suggests; yet both as Prime Minister and party leader his methods were highly unpredictable. In the course of a very long political life, he underwent many transformations, even reversals. The 'stern, unbending Tory' who opposed the 1832 Reform Act become the apostle of the new creed of liberal emancipation and free trade in the 1850s and 1860s, and the leader of an increasingly radical popular front in his later years. The champion of *laissez-faire* and public retrenchment significantly expanded the role of government in Britain, and especially in Ireland. The 'out and out egalitarian' became 'the people's William' of Midlothian days and a hero of labour. The classic Anglican defender of church establishment became a champion of the civic equality of Roman Catholics and Nonconformists. The staunch unionist was to advocate national equality for Wales and Scotland, and to stake his future on Home Rule for Ireland. The 'little Englander' who attacked imperial expansion was also to preside over major British penetration in southern Africa and the occupation of Egypt. The advocate of cosmic, universal synthesis and 'the public law' became widely associated with dissolution, fragmentation and conflict. Contemporaries found him alternately infuriating and inspiring. Yet his influence lived on long after his death. The Liberal Party rallied around Gladstonian 'guiding principles' until the 1930s, while Labour pioneers like Hardie, Henderson and Snowden viewed Gladstone as one of their heroes. In the later twentieth century, the Conservative Party claimed to be the vehicle for Gladstonian values.

Clarity and objectivity in analysing and explaining Gladstone's views and career are provided by Dr Ramm. She lays much emphasis on his intellectual and religious development, and the influence upon him of doctrines of 'approximation and adaptation' originally derived from Aristotle. She notes the major transition in his outlook in the early 1850s when he became the champion of post-Peelite Liberalism, a force for populism and for change, and the further impact of concern for nationalism and self-determination later in that crucial decade. She examines the importance of franchise reform in 1866–67 and Gladstone's handling of his vital first administration with its extraordinary legislative record. She notes also the new popular dimension foreshadowed by the agitation over the Eastern Question in the 1870s, his complex relationship with contemporaries ranging from Disraeli to Chamberlain, the major new shift in policy towards Ireland and Egypt in 1882, and the shadow cast over his last years by Irish Home Rule. His concern with a changing international scene is also shown, while constant attention is paid, too, to his incessant, restless concern with history, literature, the classical world and theological dispute. We learn of the creative chancellor, the hard-working administrator, the popular demagogue, and the devoted husband, brother and family man. As presented here, Gladstone emerges as a pragmatic, adaptable political leader, but also a towering influence who dominated his world as 'a great Christian statesman'.

Kenneth O. Morgan
The Queen's College, Oxford

Acknowledgements

It is not easy to record precisely where all one's gratitude is due in writing a little book at the end of a long reading and teaching career. I have done my best in the notes to acknowledge my sources for particular facts and views. Here I should say that this book could not have been written had the *Gladstone Diaries* not been published nor without the work of M.R.D. Foot and H.C.G. Matthew. To the latter's introductions my debt is patent. I am grateful to the Longman Group Limited for permission to use material and, where necessary, to reproduce the wording of my reviews of successive volumes in the *English Historical Review*. I am similarly grateful for permission to use material already used in my contributions to *Gladstone, Politics and Religion* (ed. Peter J. Jagger, Macmillan and St. Martin's Press, 1985) and *British Foreign Secretaries and Foreign Policy* (ed. Keith M. Wilson, Croom Helm, 1987). Naomi Sharman typed the final version with complete tolerance of my disorderly typing and a professionalism that could not make a typing error.

1

Childhood, Youth and Tory
Political Career

1809–1851

William Ewart Gladstone was born on 29 December 1809. His life was unusual in its length. He died at the age of eighty-eight years and four months, on 19 May 1898. His life thus spanned nearly the whole of the nineteenth century with all its social, intellectual and political changes. He had some part, often a decisive one, in all of them. At twenty-six he was already a junior minister, though for less than four months. He was five times Chancellor of the Exchequer and four times Prime Minister. He published at least five notable books and innumerable articles on political, religious and literary subjects. Thus his life was unusual, not because he was a noble or even pleasant character, but because he was extraordinarily able, active and courageous. Finally his life was unusual because of its unusual shape. If the normal shape of a life is like some sort of hill with an upward slope to a peak point of achievement or enjoyment and a downward slope of decline, long or short, towards its end, his was different in having two breaks, no easily discernible peak and hardly a decline, for he was eighty-four when last Prime Minister. His adult life was like a road that twice breaks off and then continues in the same direction but with a different surface.

The house in Rodney Street, Liverpool, where Gladstone was born, was built by his father who had moved there before marrying his second wife, Anne (born Robertson, daughter of a small Scottish Highland landowner), from Bold Street in 1793.[1] John Gladstone's arrival in Liverpool six years before had been a step upwards from the corn chandlery at Leith in which he had been a partner with his father. The move to Bold Street was a social improvement on quarters over the warehouse in the trading centre of Liverpool; the move to Rodney Street was another, since it took him to the perimeter of the fast-expanding town. The last improvement was to Seaforth House in 1815, which he had built in the open country on the Mersey estuary. The family's Scottish connections were never given up but rather cultivated as time went on. John Gladstone bought an estate at Fasque in Kincardineshire in 1829.

William was the fourth son and youngest-but-one child of a family of six. The family began with a daughter, Anne (died 1829) and ended with another daughter, Helen (died 1880), who came nearest to William in intellectual ability but was largely frustrated. Tom filled the role of eldest son in a patriarchal tradition, remodelled to suit the social level the Gladstones had now reached. Eton, Christ Church, the House of Commons, the inheritance of the estate at Fasque and the baronetcy, which his father had received in 1846, followed each other without much eventfulness. He died in 1889, a Tory to the end. Robertson, of gigantic physique and independent character, was early removed from Eton, worked hard at modern studies in Glasgow, and became a prominent Liverpool businessman, living at Court Hey (a country house near Roby, then a village), a Liberal in politics and a Unitarian in religion. He died isolated and disillusioned in 1875. John Neilson early left home to be a midshipman and ended as Captain RN, a Tory country gentleman and MP for Devizes, dying in 1863. William outlived them all.

During his childhood, with his mother often ill and his father always busy, William was left much to himself, to the servants and latterly to his sister Anne. There was little intellectual stimulus, plenty of material comfort and much care for being good and kind. The day, apart from lessons and excursions, was normally spent out of doors, walking, riding, observing. The religious base of Gladstone's nature was derived from his mother and the strongest influence in keeping it firm during boyhood and early manhood was that of his sister, Anne. His father, who had built and endowed two churches with schools attached to them (St Andrew's in Renshaw Street and St Thomas's at Seaforth), was more worldly but conformed to the family practice and language, which were evangelical. This meant, in practice, simple prayer, morning and evening, much reliance on the Scriptures and in church on the sermon, constant and natural acts of charity and the sense of life being lived always in the eye of God. It meant, in language, a vocabulary in which the words Providence, sin, conscience, conversion, atonement, salvation and judgement were important. The tone was not particularly intellectual, theological or even devotional, but serious, practical and constant. The political superstructure of Gladstone's nature was built by his father very early. John Gladstone had organized the victory of George Canning, candidate for Liverpool in the general election of 1812, and Canning became his friend and guest in Rodney Street and at Seaforth House. Thenceforward politics were part of the fabric of life there. They were the politics of a West Indies merchant defending his interests against the commercial policy of Lord Liverpool's Ministry (1812-27) and those of an autocratic man who 'got things done' and found popular agitation for parliamentary or other reform 'bad for business'. John Gladstone was Tory MP for the corrupt freeman borough of Lancaster (1818-20) and for the pocket borough of Woodstock (1820-26). He never fulfilled his ambition to represent Liverpool. He acquired a London base and ever-enlarging West Indian interests as he steadily climbed his way to being the millionaire he was when he died in 1851.

By 1816 John Gladstone owned the plantation 'Success' in Demerara, which he turned over to sugar production. He acquired another large estate, 'Vreedenhoop', and had mortgages on others. He also had properties in Jamaica. His sugar production per acre outdid that of other producers. He was a very large slave owner and opposed slave emancipation, taking his stand instead on the improvement of the slaves' condition. All this property was managed through agents, who were difficult to control from a distance, and did not necessarily report accurately on anything but profits and production, if on those. From December 1831 to April 1832 the slaves in Jamaica were certainly in insurrection. In 1833 William Gladstone had already followed his brother Tom into Parliament, and had found the defence of his father's treatment of his slaves one of his earliest concerns.

His childhood had ended when in 1821 he was sent to Eton. He was now a boy going through the difficulties of adolescence and taking them somewhat heavily. At Eton he learnt to work—of his own initiative, for there was no special stimulus. He learnt a good command of his own language through the constant construing from Latin and Greek and constant exercise in classical prosody. He learnt French as an 'extra' (he was later to learn, with little tuition, Italian and German) and read quite a lot of Molière and Racine. He was confirmed into the Church of England. The school's religious life was far removed from the evangelical 'enthusiasm' of his family, but its impersonality enabled a boy to read into it what he wished. From 1825 he was already keeping the diary into which he continued to make daily entries until a few

months before his death.[2] Already as a fifth-form boy he was a member
of the 'Eton Society', a select group meeting weekly to debate motions
on literary and historical subjects—history interpreted as past politics.
He moved in a set of some dozen friends, whose friendship he retained
through life. There was one friend closer than the rest, Arthur Hallam,
son of the historian Henry Hallam, and later the subject of Tennyson's
In Memoriam. There was, of course, no formal instruction in English
literature or History, but no shortage of opportunities for reading and
writing: in his last year Gladstone was editing a magazine, the *Eton
Miscellany,* in which he wrote as Bartholomew Bouverie. He left the
school he loved on 2 December 1827.

A young man of eighteen, he went to a private tutor, the Revd
J.M. Turner of Wilmslow, Cheshire, to read some of the texts he would
need in Oxford—Juvenal and Homer—and much mathematics. In April
1828 he went back to his family, temporarily living in Edinburgh. In
October he went up to Christ Church, Oxford. He had been in Oxford
or nearby since August. The tutors responsible for directing his reading
and for private tuition there were Augustus Page Saunders, later Dean
of Peterborough, and Robert Biscoe. He was immensely hard-working,
reading, when in spate, some eight to ten hours a day. The diary enables
one to follow him through the Greek and Latin historians, through the
logic syllabus and the *Ethics* of Aristotle, the Greek dramatists and, in
Latin literature, Juvenal (a wise tutor put him first on to Johnson's
imitation of the thirteenth satire in *The Vanity of Human Wishes)* and
Lucretius. He was following the normal classical syllabus, but he was
reading much mathematics in parallel and many books outside the
recommended texts. He never lost the habit of keeping two or three,
sometimes five or six, books in reading simultaneously or of making
analyses and summaries of what he read. Some of the self-
disparagement already characteristic of the diary was clearly an
incitement to more work. He duly went down from Oxford with first-
class honours both in classics and mathematics in December 1831,
having postponed for a term the examinations for his degree in order
to excel in this way.

He was immensely ambitious. Very early he determined to take all
the possible university prizes. Against his tutor's advice and with no
encouragement from his friends, he was already in his first year a
competitor for the Ireland and the Craven scholarships. But he never
won either, nor the All Souls Fellowship for which he also tried. He
was runner-up for the Ireland in his last year and was made a Student

(i.e. Fellow) of Christ Church but had no other formal academic recognition before his degree. Ambition was political as well as academic. He was early a member of the Union where the literary and historical motions for debate were all essentially political. There was less disguise in the essay society he founded (The WEG) which met each Saturday evening in term, two essays being read one week and discussed the next. When in 1831 the excitement over the Reform Bill erupted, Gladstone's commitment against it was public and striking. He placarded the town; he canvassed for, and procured signatures to, a petition from the resident MAs and undergraduates which was duly presented to Parliament; he spoke for three-quarters of an hour in the Union against it (17 May 1831).

Finally, he was notably religious. But he was not to be won as a disciple by H.B. Bulteel, the leading evangelical parson in Oxford, nor by St Edmund Hall, the centre of an evangelical group, nor in his last year, though he was given one of the Tracts and heard Newman, by the Tractarians. He attended chapel as he was obliged to do, and at one time kept the roll of chapel absentees; he went regularly to the University Sermon and to many other University religious occasions. He was a regular communicant—but oddly noted again and again how few or many undergraduates were present, expressing appropriate regret or pleasure. His ecclesiastical practice was conventional, regular and conformist. His private religious life as recorded in the diary was intense, self-depreciatory and exacting. His rescue work among 'women of the streets' had begun already in Oxford.[3] Nevertheless, despite work, ambition and religious assiduity, he was no insufferable prig. The occasion when a group of roisterers burst into his rooms and beat him up suggests that some men thought he was. But he was quite ordinary in enjoying Oxford, furnishing and embellishing his rooms, inviting friends to wine and going to their parties, talking into the small hours, walking or riding into the countryside, listening to music, playing or singing himself, dining once in a while with the Dean or a tutor. He was only out of the ordinary in that all his activity was deliberate, planned and recorded.

It is thought by some that Gladstone passed through a crisis in Oxford: a crisis of choice between a career in the Church or in politics. When Tom visited him during his first term William spoke to him of his wish for the former. Tom spoke to their father and passed on the father's sensible view that it was William's decision and should not be taken in a hurry. On 4 August 1830 William wrote to his father an extraordinarily laboured and prolix letter detailing the reasons why he wished for a career in the Church.[4] John Gladstone replied much as before. On 17 January 1832, after the Reform Bill excitement, William wrote to his father in a different vein. He would serve his cause, for cause he must have, in the State rather than the Church. There was no real battle of wills between father and son, no real clash between the mother's piety and the businessman's outlook of the father, nor even a struggle between two elements in Gladstone's nature. There was something factitious in that long letter. The religious foundation of his nature and the political superstructure upon it were to exist throughout his life. The last word on this topic may rest with John Morley; 'the impulse [towards the clerical profession] in its first shape did not endure, but in essence, it never faded'.[5]

After Oxford, Gladstone, with his brother John and John's dog Banker,[6] made a continental tour. It lasted from 1 February to 28 July 1832. From Ostend they went to Antwerp, Brussels, Paris, through Savoy, across the Alps, to Turin through the valleys of the Waldenses (the subject of Milton's sonnet 'Avenge, O Lord, . . .') to Genoa, Pisa, Florence, Siena, Rome, Naples, Vesuvius, Paestum, Amalfi, Sorrento, back by way of various classical sites to Rome, Venice, Milan, Lausanne, Geneva, the Rhine valley to Cologne, Aix-la-Chapelle, Brussels and so home. It was a rich man's tour, sometimes by carriage, sometimes by diligence or post-chaise, but also that of an essentially reflective, observing, active-minded man. They had taken with them a sufficiency of books: Pitt's and Fox's *Speeches*, Coleridge's translation of Schiller's *Wallenstein*, Pascal's *Provincial Letters*, Bossuet's *Funeral Orations*, some half dozen tourists' guides. Sightseeing included churches, libraries and picture galleries ('But I never had any discrimination in pictures').[7] There was much singing and some singing lessons and a great deal of language learning. There was also a considerable broadening of religious horizons. Gladstone had begun to move away from the evangelical position before going up to Oxford. In the spring of 1828 his mind was full of thoughts on baptism. He discussed it with his sister, Anne, and with the Revd Edward Craig of Edinburgh—a Calvinist. We know from a letter to his sister Helen (24 August 1828) that by then he had come to believe that baptism was more than a sign that the child had entered into the religious inheritance of its parents (the evangelical position) but was indeed the means by which the child received God's grace and was born again, born into the spiritual life. A second step away from the evangelicals may be reflected in his correspondence from Oxford with his sister, Anne, on the subject of conversion. After months spent in Roman Catholic countries on his tour he took a further step. The first effect of visiting the churches was a superficial and inconclusive discussion with himself about the worship of images. The last effect was a reading of those often unread parts of the *Book of Common Prayer*. The outcome was the supersession in his mind of the importance of the relationship between God and the individual (as the evangelicals thought of it) by the importance of the relationship between God and the universal Church of which the individual was only part.[8] The full effects were to be seen in 1838.

Meanwhile, on 6 July, at Milan, had occurred 'the most remarkable day of my life'.[9] Gladstone recorded with this phrase his receiving a letter from his Eton friend, Lord Lincoln, inviting him to stand for Lincoln's father's borough of Newark. The expenses were to be shared by the two fathers, the Duke of Newcastle and John Gladstone, jointly. In fact, 'the treatment' of voters cost twice as much as the expected £1,000 and an argument about 'treating' went on through the thirteen years that Gladstone sat for the borough. Anyhow, Gladstone accepted from Geneva on 15 July 1832. So it was that after publishing an address, a little canvassing, much entertaining, standing on the hustings and holding out through three days' polling, Gladstone became a member of the first reformed Parliament. He was an old-fashioned Tory, sitting for an old-fashioned constituency, in a Parliament where Whigs and Radicals together had a majority of over three hundred. From 29 January 1833 until he resigned his premiership on 3 March 1894, that is for the next sixty-one years, with one interval of a year and seven months, he was a regular attender at the House of Commons, and as regularly recorded the hours he spent there, the divisions he voted in and the important speeches he made, often their length. He continued MP until the dissolution of 1895 but no longer attended. He made his maiden speech on Monday, 3 June, defending for fifty minutes his father's West Indian estates from Lord Howick's imputations during the debate on the Slave Emancipation Bill. He spoke a second time on the same subject and three more times on other topics during July.

He was now living in the Albany, off Piccadilly, the recognized place for ambitious and wealthy young bachelors; he had entered at Lincoln's Inn on 25 January and was to keep thirteen terms there, dining pretty frequently until 1839; he was a member of the Oxford and Cambridge Club (1833–42); he was elected to the Carlton on 7 March 1833 and did not let his subscription lapse until 1860; he was elected to Grillions dining club on 31 January 1840; finally, and a sign that he had 'arrived', he was elected to The Club (founded by Dr Johnson) on 21 April 1857.

Gladstone's readiness and point as a speaker attracted Sir Robert Peel's attention, and when Peel formed his first Government after William IV's dismissal of the Whig Lord Melbourne, he made Gladstone a Junior Lord of the Treasury (20 December 1834). The vicissitudes of the general election which followed enabled Peel to promote him to be Parliamentary Under-Secretary for the Colonies (26 January). Since Lord Aberdeen, the Colonial Secretary, was in the Lords, Gladstone spoke for all colonial concerns in the Commons. He lost office, of course, with the rest of this minority government, on 7 April 1835. What he was principally at this time was a hard-working committee man. The select committees on which he served ranged from the humdrum and dull, such as those on the Bedford or the Ipswich Election or the Glasgow Lottery or that on the Inns of Court decision against D. Whittle Harvey becoming a barrister, to those requiring special knowledge and developing his particular expertise. These latter related to colonial affairs (colonial apprentices, land-distribution in New Zealand, the conduct of the Governor General of New South Wales, the treatment of natives by British settlers, the South African Aborigines Committee); and to education and the Church (Irish Education and especially the system of mixed-denominational schools set up in 1831, national education, the working of Queen Anne's Bounty). One interesting foreshadowing of the future was his service, year in, year out, on the Speaker's Committee for the Library of the House of Commons.[10] Gladstone was later to be a founder member of the London Library, to write at the end of his life on the shelving of books and to leave his mark on the book stacks of Bodley's Library in Oxford.[11]

Of these areas of interest it was finance which eventually predominated. Peel determined this; for when he made his second Government, after the general election of 1841 had given the Tories a majority, he offered Gladstone the Vice-Presidency of the Board of Trade under Lord Ripon. Gladstone was disappointed, but Peel had judged right; among facts and figures, Gladstone's ability and industry would bring him irresistibly to the top and he would be a political asset. In any other place, where general ideas might find more scope, Gladstone's speculative bent and his religious views might hold him back, might indeed make him ridiculous and he would be no political asset. Gladstone seems himself to have scented the danger. In anticipation of some offer he was afraid of being 'bewildered by imagination on one side . . . or even a *general* desire to serve the country on the other'.[12] Despite his disappointment, he accepted and so it was that in the field of finance lay Gladstone's main achievement in life. In his junior position Gladstone's reputation was already made because of the assistance he gave Peel in the tariff changes for which the budget of 1842 was memorable. Then when Ripon died Gladstone succeeded (May 1843) to the Presidency of the Board of Trade and became a member of the Cabinet.

There we may leave the practical and political side of him to say something of his speculations and of the religious development which culminated in the book of 1838. Though by 1835, as described above, he had left the evangelical position, he retained from it his intense consciousness of sin. The note of self-disparagement in his diary is insistent. When it appeared in public it could, in such a successful man, be caricatured as ridiculous hypocrisy. Among the themes which run through the set of essays he wrote on speculative and religious subjects between 1835 and 1837, the strongest is that of the fallibility or sinfulness of all men. On this subject, he believed he held a middle position. On one side was the extreme Protestant and Lutheran playing down of inherent sinfulness, along with the exaggeration of man's guilt (or failure to do something about it). On the other side was the Roman exaggeration of inherent sinfulness and playing down of man's guilt. He stood between. He believed he had absorbed the teaching of Pascal: 'It is dangerous to let a man see too clearly how much he has in common with the animals, without at the same time making him realise his greatness. It is also dangerous to let him see his greatness too clearly, without realising his baseness'.[13] The second theme of these early essays was the will. He thought of it as a faculty which a man could use to determine which of his desires should eventuate in action. For himself he would seek to understand what was the commandment of his creator for him, and use his will to conform his action to it. He repeatedly quoted from Dante *In la sua voluntade e nostra pace* (In God's will lies our peace). The third theme was the place of reason in relation to religion. By nineteenth-century controversialists it was called the place in religion of 'private judgement'. Gladstone claimed that it was the peculiar glory of the Church of England (which distinguished it from the Church of Rome) to allow room for reason as well as authority. But reason must operate only within the bounds of the ideas given by revelation—to argue from true premises to true conclusions not to disprove the premises. At the point where it seemed to conflict with revelation it was false and must stop.[14]

Gladstone drew support from his reading of Aristotle. In a later article he recounts how Aristotle, in book six of the *Ethics*, distinguishes between *scientific knowledge* or knowledge about things that are not variable, that is, are eternal, having no end and no beginning, being neither made nor done, and *intuitive reason*, or the instrument which enables an individual to grasp first principles. Gladstone then went on to show that Aristotle distinguishes both of these from the *calculative faculty*, which, working on variable things, that is, things made or done, leads on to practical wisdom. To this discussion Gladstone then reconciled his own distinction between reason, Aristotle's calculative faculty, which works from any arbitrarily chosen variable, to new conclusions, and reason, Aristotle's intuitive reason completed by scientific knowledge, which works from a given invariable so as to understand it rather than draw new conclusions. He strengthened his belief by referring to Coleridge's use of the German distinction between *Vernunft* and *Verstand:* reason to argue and reason to understand. He had read Coleridge's *On the Constitution of the Church and State* (1830) in 1837.[15] Its influence is strong in Gladstone's book, *The State in its Relations with the Church* (1838). This had a mixed reception and, from Macaulay, a devastating review.[16] It was the last serious work to claim that the English State was identical with the English Church. He republished it with additions and explanations in 1841, but never repudiated its main argument. In 1840 he published a second book, *Church Principles,* in which he developed the ideas sketched out in the early essays.

The weakness in the 1839 book upon which Macaulay had pounced was a failure to prove his essential contention that the State was an organism and moreover a moral organism with a knowledge of good and evil. Gladstone maintained that the morality of the State was shown in the morality of the law of the State. He conveys a strong sense of the living quality of relationships within the State, but he is descriptive rather than fully logical. He maintains that the State and the Church have a common area in the religion of the State in relation to which the one has executive and the other originative functions. This could be said of any religion or of any Church, but his final position is that it can, in England, only be said of what he now comes to call 'the national Church'. He reaches this position by an historical narrative and not a logical argument. He begins with the making of the established Church in the reign of Elizabeth and leaves the reader in no doubt that it gained from being an established Church for it attracted to religion the power of nationality. Then he recounts the history of religious toleration until it was 'finally affirmed that differences in religious opinion have no bearing upon the discharge of political and social duties'.[17] But he does not, therefore, identify the English State with a State of many religions or many Churches, but identifies the State of England with the Church of England. He was doing two irreconcilable things—taking his stand on England's member-ship of the universal Church and taking his stand on a national Church. He never in the book reconciled the two positions.

Gladstone could only reconcile them by the doctrines of approxima-tion and adaptation which the early essays show him to have drawn from Aristotle's *Politics.* Aristotle's teleology depended on an idea of the perfect which men strove after but in the actual world never attained. The perfect constitution was the ideal polity where all ruled all. In the actual circumstances in which men lived they put up with an approxima-tion, as we might say, and adapted the ideal to what was possible. These doctrines of approximation and adaptation were to have political consequences throughout Gladstone's life.

Finally, in 1831 he had discovered Bishop Butler.[18] In 1845 he began to work on an edition of the *Analogy of Religion* first published in 1736, and eventually, in 1896, he republished it. Gladstone had already adopted the 'probableism' which he was to develop and apply to every political circumstance for the rest of his life. 'Why,' he once asked, 'should anyone be content with presumptive evidence that the food he eats will not poison him or the horse he chooses will not break his neck, yet demand complete certainty, absolute truth in religion?' Butler was to strengthen Gladstone in never demanding complete certainty, in always adapting his ideals and beliefs to the best that could be done or believed in the circumstances. Approximation and adaptation explain the empiricism which marked Gladstone's career until its last Home Rule phase when it seemed to disappear.

By now he had married and acquired a family. His courtship of Caroline Farquhar, who considered him to be too serious, failed in 1835–6. His mother had died at Fasque in September 1835 and both Tom and Robertson married during 1835–6. Gladstone's second courtship failed in 1838. Lady Frances Douglas also found him too earnest. With Catherine Glynne he succeeded and they were married on 25 July 1839. His wife belonged to the old political aristocracy as well as to the Anglo-Welsh country gentry. His success in winning her owed something to the lighter atmosphere of happiness and excitement during his second Italian journey. There had been four hundred miles of mule-back travelling in Sicily as well as much sightseeing and social life in Naples and Rome, where he met her. It was she who brought their life to Hawarden Castle on the Welsh border, where she had been born in 1812 and which became her brother's property. Their eldest son, William, was born in 1840, Agnes in 1842, Stephen in 1844. Jessie and Mary followed in 1845 and 1847. There were three more children: Helen, Henry and Herbert, less overshadowed by their parents' lives. Catherine Glynne was a gifted and talented woman who took life with great assurance and complete serenity. She had organizing ability which she applied to large households in London and Hawarden and to her many charities, notably the Clewer House of Refuge. She had considerable independence of mind. She was said to think and speak 'in stepping stones', an art she may well have cultivated to evade unwanted confrontations and as a means of keeping the political secrets which her husband, with absolute and justified confidence in her discretion, confided without restraint to her.[19]

From high philosophic speculation or the unpredictable trifles of family life, Gladstone turned to the dry, grey business of the Board of Trade. 'I have been talking about Hops, Soap, Cordage . . . and other matters till I am wearied and am determined to go and walk round the water in the park.'[20] This was written to Catherine at six o'clock on a Saturday afternoon when he was still at the office. He was there daily from twelve to seven or later and at the House of Commons afterwards. His period at the Board of Trade was immensely important. Gladstonian Liberalism is unthinkable without free trade. It was now that free trade was step by step introduced into the British commercial system by Gladstone under Peel. In this way he laid the foundations of Gladstonian Liberalism when he was at the Board of Trade.

In 1841 the tariffs were so intricate that only customs officers, exporters and importers knew what they were, and they only each in his own line. It was not possible for any single man to know the tariff map of Britain. Between 1841 and 1845, this was pretty nearly what Gladstone succeeded in doing, and what enabled him to carry his views in contention with civil servants, his superiors and the House of Commons. There were 1,200 articles on the tariff but ninety per cent of the revenue was brought in by duties on imported corn, sugar, timber and a few other things, including coffee. The first three were contentious subjects but all were lowered. In addition, the export duties on raw wool (needed for home industry) and coal were first lowered and then in 1845 abolished, except for a small coal duty retained for revenue. The export duty on machinery was abolished in 1843 and British inventions became freely available to Belgian and German entrepreneurs. Altogether duties on 123 things and categories of things were abolished and on 133 they were reduced.[21]

The two new tariffs of 1842 and 1845, when keyed together and fully applied, were a successful demonstration that lower duties ultimately provided a larger revenue but, before the results could build up, some compensation had to be found for an immediate contraction of revenue. This Peel proposed to find by imposing a new income tax, based on the taxpayer's own return of his income under four schedules: land, investments, salaries and profits of trade. Gladstone, through his chief, Lord Ripon, proposed a property or house tax. Ripon was not equal to making an informed opinion on the subject and Gladstone was brought into direct argument with Peel. Direct relations continued and so when Gladstone replaced Ripon as President, with a seat in the Cabinet, there was little change in the partnership with Peel. In 1842 Peel, with Goulbourn's assistance from the Exchequer, out-argued Gladstone. The income tax was imposed and Gladstone defended it in the House of Commons.

The corn duties were another source of contention. These were levied on a sliding scale, duty going down as price went up, to admit foreign corn at a low duty when the home price was high. Gladstone worked until he mastered the expertise of averaging out the price of corn over the whole country, on which the fixing of duty depended. He provided a scale with certain 'rests' where the duty stayed the same over several rises in price. Peel produced a scale with the 'rests' differently placed and shorter, and the upper limit at a different point.[22] Gladstone fought for his scale, deploying all his detailed knowledge against Peel to the point of threatening resignation. It was only later that he recognized his mistake: one did not threaten a government except on a matter of principle.[23] At this point he was dissuaded by Peel. Anyhow, Peel's corn law with its easier sliding scale only lasted until the ports had to be opened in December 1845 because of the Irish famine, and in 1846 it was repealed. Meanwhile, Gladstone's combined study of gambling on the averages and of Ricardo's theory of rent, together with his realization of the advantages of bringing the rich untilled lands of Canada into cultivation, had brought him by 1845 to believe in free trade.

The two acts dealing with the sugar duties of 1844 and 1845 were also the joint work of Gladstone and Peel but caused less contention between them. They were a difficult subject because they involved three separate interests: (1) the consumer, (2) the West Indies planters, who found the apprentice system an inadequate replacement for slave labour, and could no longer get an adequate return on their capital, and (3) the humanitarians who wished to keep the duty on Brazilian or slave-grown sugar higher than that on sugar grown by free labour. In the end duties were so lowered as to reduce the price to the consumer by 1½d. a pound, the apprenticeship system was abolished and a slight differential maintained.

Peel and Gladstone together had shifted, in principle and in principle only, the basis of British taxation from indirect to direct taxes. But income tax levied at 7d. in the £ on incomes over £150 p.a. brought in, in 1850–52, £5–£5½ million p.a. and other direct taxes and the stamp duties £11 million, while customs duties still brought in £20-£21 million p.a.[24]

At the Board of Trade Gladstone was also engaged in negotiating commercial treaties with Spain and Portugal and was responsible for the substance of three more acts of Parliament and for working them through the House. His Railway Act of 1842 increased the powers of the Railway Department at the Board of Trade, which he organized, to arbitrate between rival companies and to inspect and control railways in the interest and for the convenience and safety of passengers. His act of 1844 provided for third-class travel at a uniform rate of 1d. a mile on all railways, with one cheap through train (the parliamentary train) on all lines every day. The most interesting provisions, cut out during the act's passage, would have provided for eventual purchase of the railways by the State—nationalization. Gladstone's third act, introduced in April 1844, regulated the joint-stock companies, exploiting the device of registration to enable investors to know with whom they were dealing and to have appropriate remedies for deception. It paved the way for the limited-liability company.

Gladstone's office labour diminished a little, from the daily six hours or more when it began, first to five and then after 1843 to less; in proportion as his office work dropped his parliamentary labour increased—he records 156 divisions in 1845—and Cabinet work was now added. Then in 1844–45 came the crisis over Maynooth.[25] On 28 January 1845 Gladstone resigned from Peel's Government. It was an individual act and not on a main issue such as the corn law would have been in 1842. Since, moreover, the ground for it was well known to be personal consistency and not substantive opposition—he subsequently voted with the Government for the increased grant to the Catholic College at Maynooth in Ireland—his resignation had no effect on the Government. Since 1838, Gladstone's standing for the idea that the single English Church was the same thing as the single English State was a matter of public notoriety. This position was reinforced by his opposition to the education clauses, which failed to provide for Anglican religious instruction, of Graham's factory bill. He could not with consistency ('the public may very fairly regard me as a mere adventurer, if I should part company with character'[26]) then remain part of a government which increased a state grant to a college for educating Catholic clergy. He then voted as a private member for the increase by adapting his ideal to actual circumstances wherein the only way to govern a Catholic country was to help educate its clergy. Gladstone's doctrines of approximation and adaptation had shown their political implications.

From January until the end of December 1845 he was without official employment. This made little difference to his non-political activities. His career as a man of letters began in 1842 and his first group of ten articles was published between 1843 and 1847, not much affected by whether he was in or out of office. Indeed his first articles were rooted in public controversy rather than in his private bookish life—as were contributions to the *Liverpool Standard* which began soon after he went down from Oxford. They were three articles contributed to the *Foreign and Colonial Quarterly Review*, a new periodical edited by the Revd James Worthington. The first reviewed a number of parliamentary papers and the Prussian *Zollverein* tariff just published (January 1843); the second was on 'The present aspect of the Church' (September 1843); the third reviewed *The Theses of Erastus touching Excommunication translated with a preface by Dr Lea* (October 1844). The articles were anonymous (though their author was quickly recognized), virtually unpaid and written on subjects of his choice. They originated in his urge to systematize and record. Worthington's review ceased publication in 1846.[27] Meanwhile, Gladstone had written two articles, also anonymous, of a wholly literary character in another new and relatively short-lived review. For the first number of the *English Review* (April 1844) he wrote what he called 'a paltry criticism' of Lord John Russell's translation of the Paolo and Francesca story in Dante's *Inferno,* comparing it with the versions of Cary, of Dayman and of Byron. For the second number, he wrote a review of *Ellen Middleton,* a Tractarian novel in three volumes, by Lady Georgiana Fullerton, of which the central idea was the need to confess one's misdeeds. He discusses plot and character-drawing rather than its Tractarian position. The *English Review,* begun as a less provocative substitute for the Tractarian *British Critic,* lasted only to 1853. Gladstone already in 1844 had approached John Lockhart, and thenceforward had a regular outlet for participation in public controversy, or for literary criticism as he chose, in the *Quarterly Review* which Lockhart edited. The first contribution (December 1844) was a review of W.G. Ward's *Ideal of a Christian Church,* an article in the area of public controversy though by submitting to Lockhart's alterations he allowed its argumentative character to be softened. The next (June 1845) reviewed J.H. Thom and J.E. White, *Blanco White,* and was the first of several articles reviewing accounts of men and women living strange contorted lives under great strain. With 'Scotch ecclesiastical affairs' (December 1845) he returned to public controversy, and with the review of Elizabeth Harris's *From Oxford to Rome* (June 1847) to the Tractarian novel. Finally, with his review of Lachman's *Über die ersten zehn Bücher des Ilias* (1839) and *Fernere Betrachtungen über die Ilias* (1843) (December 1847) he entered the Homeric field to which his contributions constitute his real claim to the title of man of letters.

At the end of 1845, Peel's Government had fallen. Lord John Russell then 'handed back the poisoned chalice', Peel resumed office and appointed Gladstone Colonial Secretary. By the constitutional law as it then existed Gladstone was obliged to seek re-election. He did not seek it at Newark because he differed from the Duke of Newcastle on tariff reform and he was without a seat in Parliament from December 1845 to August 1847, when he became MP for Oxford University.[28] Gladstone's administration of colonial affairs was important because his characteristic generalizing and systematizing habit of mind led him to develop a colonial theory. Again characteristically, the theory was recorded. A despatch to Lord Cathcart, Governor-General of Canada, 3 February 1846, contains part of his doctine, but most of it is to be found in an incomplete draft of a pamphlet on colonial policy written in 1848–49.[29] The theory was important because it was adhered to by a group of men, Peelites, who themselves became Colonial Secretaries in later years: the Duke of Newcastle (until 1851 Lord Lincoln), his Eton and Christ Church friend, Colonial Secretary 1852–54; Sidney Herbert, Colonial Secretary 1855; and Edward Cardwell, Colonial Secretary

1864–66. From this Peelite group the ideas were transmitted into the body of views that made up Gladstonian Liberalism which was never anti-imperial, though equally never 'imperialist' in the Disraelian sense.

According to Gladstone's theory, free trade and the repeal of the Navigation Acts (1849) having ended the commercial advantages which Britain and her colonies had once mutually enjoyed, their belonging together must now depend on feeling, common outlook and early protection, on intangibles not on calculable, quantifiable things. 'We cannot stamp the image of England on the colonies', he wrote, 'like a coat of arms upon wax. For all true, genuine, wholesome and permanent resemblance, we must depend upon a law written not upon stone, but on the fleshy table of the heart'.[30] He described the connection between Britain and Canada as 'founded upon . . . protection rendered from the one side, and allegiance freely and loyally returned from the other, upon the common traditions of the past, and hopes for the future, upon resemblances in origins, in laws and in manners, in what inwardly binds men and communities of men together'.[31] Secondly, Gladstone believed in colonial self-government. 'Our fellow subjects in the colonies,' he said in 1848, 'ought to be able truly to manage their own affairs and ought to have constitutional guarantees for the security of that liberty'.[32] He planned the elective Chamber for New Zealand, enacted by his successor later in 1846, and also supported the Australian Colonies Government Bill of 1849 (4 June) and the amended Bill of February 1850. He disliked nominated members of single-chamber parliaments and nominated upper houses of two-chamber constitutions.

Thirdly, he believed the colonies should pay their own administrative and military expenses. Self-defence was the natural corollary of self-government. But there were parts of this subject that only became clear with time and then the narrow distinction he drew between the colonies' domestic concerns and the safety of the empire as a whole which must be reserved for the Crown and Imperial Parliament, could not always be easily applied. Fourthly, he thought immigration from Britain into the colonies should be encouraged if only to increase the labour-supply. He was, of course, especially impressed with the labour problems of the sugar plantations in the West Indies. But he supported Wakefield's plan of State-aided colonization. He always disliked the Hudson Bay Company because it exploited national and colonial interests alike, for profit from the fur trade. Finally, he considered that Britain should assist the colonies to thrive economically and to develop peaceful relations with existing populations whose culture and religion the colony must respect. In 1847 he spoke in defence of the land rights of the Maoris in New Zealand. He supported a scheme extracted from the Government for a guaranteed loan in aid of public works in the West Indies (1848). As Prime Minister, Gladstone went back on none of these doctrines, though he developed some in ways which were only justifiable by doctrines of approximation to the best solutions and adaptation to actual circumstances. These ways were not easily reconciled by plain men with his claims to be consistent.

During this period as a young man, from his marriage to the spring of 1842, he was essentially happy — confident, planning forward, living through all the natural emotions. He was working tremendously hard, missing wife and son when away, spending happy mornings with them before going off to the office at mid-day, to return home after Parliament at midnight. It is all normal though the pace was more intense and the events and emotions more often recorded than usual. But in 1842 his fortress began to be assailed. First, in May his sister Helen became a Roman Catholic. She lived unmarried in her father's house at Fasque. She was to have recourse more and more to the opium-based laudanum, much prescribed at this period, and to alcoholic stimulants and to be increasingly liable to neurotic seizures. Gladstone was to understand that she was ill and eccentric, because she had no acceptable outlet for energies and intellect as active and strong as his own,[33] but he was quite without mercy in condemning her behaviour. Once very fond of him, she came to hate and fear him in return. There was a scene over drugs in October 1844 and Helen went off to Germany on 20 July 1845. After various vicissitudes, in 1848 she was suddenly cured. But her very recovery carried seeds of fresh trouble, because it was proclaimed a miracle and made much of.

In the late autumn of 1842 (13 September) at Hawarden, Gladstone shot off the top joint of the forefinger of his left hand and the rest of the finger was removed. Thenceforward he wore a finger stall. It was a shock to him and to Catherine but the wound healed quickly and was forgotten in the return to London and the resumption of work at the Board of Trade. Soon after the birth of Agnes, Gladstone noted for the first time in his diary (31 October 1842) a rescue case by name. 'Saw the girl Rebecca [Ayscough] — the visit was satisfactory.' The reader of the diary comes to recognize an increase in the frequency of such entries as signs of strain. At this date they were rare and it was two years before he had recourse again to that kind of relief.

The birthday review of the year (29 December 1843) is the first to strike an obsessive note: obsession with his own sin. 'Another year of my life is closed', he writes, '& again I have before me the awful question, what is the state of the soul before God, & what movement has there been in that state? . . . Fearful is the guilt of sin returning again & again in forms ever new but alike hideous; always some fresh pretext for admission, always the same stain upon the soul . . .' The entry for 29 December 1844 was happier but thenceforward the annual balance sheet struck on birthday or New Year's Eve constantly shows Gladstone's sense of sin − a general awareness before God of his own shortcomings, never a confession of particular sins. Meanwhile throughout 1844 and until he resigned in January 1845 he was at tension over Maynooth. Relaxation of pressure now that he was without office work was almost harder to bear than the daily grind. The fear of not making good use of the precious gift of time obsessed him; for in February 1845 he took 'the engagement of discipline' with T.D. Acland and his brother, F. Rogers, R. Palmer and nine others.[34] The tight rules which they imposed on themselves involved not only church attendance and observance of fast days, some regular work of charity and mutual supervision, but caused Gladstone, if not the others, to record each day the number of hours spent in recreation, meals and sleep. This negative record was changed on 23 August 1845. Thenceforward the figure beside each day in the diary represents the time spent on 'devotion, study and business'. With the loss of his parliamentary seat and then the fall of the Government and the end of his work at the Colonial Office, his life took a turn for the better and the figures stopped. July to December 1846 was a period of real leisure spent at Hawarden and Fasque and the review of 29 December was 'more hopeful [i.e. of moral improvement] than it has been in some former years'.

Then came another blow. Oak Farm and the attempt to save it from bankruptcy dominated 1847–48.[35] This was an estate belonging to Sir Stephen Glynne, Catherine's brother, with coal-mines and an ironworks under the management of F. Boydell. Boydell over-expanded and mortgaged more and more to find necessary capital. When the company went into liquidation at the petition of Lord Ward, one of the creditors, its liabilities were £450,000 secured on the Hawarden estate which, of course, also belonged to Sir Stephen Glynne. On 23 November 1847 the Glynnes and Gladstones withdrew their support from Boydell and he summoned the creditors. In May 1848 bankruptcy proceedings began in Birmingham. Thenceforward, Gladstone was occupied with expedients to buy back the assets of the company, including the Hawarden estate of some seven thousand acres, and to find in the interim an income for Sir Stephen Glynne. Meanwhile Gladstone was again MP. In August 1847 he had been elected for Oxford University which then, like Cambridge, sent two members to Parliament. But he complained in 1848 that Oak Farm 'made it quite impossible for me to discharge my duties properly in Parliament: but there is no escape at hand'.[36] Enough of the Hawarden estate was sold to bring in £200,000 which was used to buy back some of the company's assets. A gift of money from his father enabled Gladstone to buy half the Hawarden land. There was still a debt of a quarter of a million pounds, paid off before Sir Stephen Glynne died in 1874 except for £90,000. Gladstone was obliged to sell, at a loss, 13 Carlton House Terrace (he returned to the Terrace later but to no. 18) and move to a smaller house at 6 Carlton Gardens, and the move hurt. Hawarden Castle was not sold, but was not again lived in until 1852. He calculated that the whole proceedings cost him a third of his income. But the Oak Farm Company and the Hawarden estate were both nursed back to life. The Gladstone and the Glynne families occupied Hawarden Castle jointly between 1852 and 1874 when Sir Stephen died. Hawarden then briefly became Gladstone's property before he made it over his son, William. It passed after William's death in 1891 to his son, a minor. Gladstone and his wife continued to occupy the castle.

In the second half of 1847 came the illness of his daughter Agnes with erysipelas. It began in September at Fasque. There was a week of acute anxiety, but by 24 September she had begun to mend. Full recovery took two months and by then he himself was ill with the disease. This, as well as Oak Farm, prevented his taking advantage of his re-election to Parliament. His first speech after a silence of nearly two and a half years was on 8 December 1847 on the Catholic Relief Bill. To Oak Farm and illness was now added trouble with his father. His father at eighty-two had had a slight stroke in January 1847 from which he made a good recovery, but he became more and more demanding of his son's time as secretary, conversationalist and companion. Gladstone took himself to task for grudging this time, but he was, in fact, at Fasque autumn after autumn during the years 1847–50, a drudge. Most difficult of all was his father's drive to storm him out of his free trade convictions. To argue with him was to excite him; not to argue was to encourage him to go on hectoring. Signs of the stress of these years were the increase in rescue work, a dread of his inability to resist the fascination of mild pornography (Petronius or French *fabliaux*) and the beginning on 18 January 1849 of the use of the scourge to counteract it.

In 1849, from 13 July to 10 August, he was engaged on a three-thousand-mile journey which took him to Rome, Naples, Milan, Como, Varena, Lecco and back to Milan on the track of 'Suzie', Lady Lincoln. She was always ahead of him and got away in the end to Bergamo. The pursuit had precipitated the birth of her child, and Gladstone had obtained for his friend, Lord Lincoln, the necessary evidence for a divorce from his wife citing Lord Walpole as co-respondent. The escapade was begun with 'a very terrible blow' and the whole affair was disagreeable and to Catherine, who had been fond of Lady Lincoln, heart-rending. On 1 April 1850 Gladstone gave evidence in the divorce proceedings.

In 1850 came the illness of Catherine Jessie, not yet five years old. She was 'listless', then in March 'tediously ill', suddenly on 29 March seriously so. The ups and downs of fever and pain were appalling, for it was meningitis: she died in London on 9 April 1850. Gladstone broke down, but the controls re-asserted themselves and he found an outlet for grief in writing about her and taking her body to be buried in the vault beneath the new chapel at Fasque. Catherine took the other four children to Brighton.

In politics, Gladstone was now isolated with the small group of Peelites whom Peel refused to organize or lead while no one else could do so as long as he lived. Gladstone's discomfort was all the greater because of his admiration and his sense that Peel was the star by which he steered his own ship. On 29 June 1850 Peel was thrown from his horse; three days later, 2 July, he died. 'The great calamity which the nation has suffered in the death of its greatest statesman'[37] was a personal as well as a national disaster. Meanwhile, on 11 December 1850 Sir John Gladstone had become eighty-six. His powers were failing and he was often confused, but his will and his domination were unimpaired. On Sunday, 7 December 1851, he died after a series of slight strokes. The tale of disasters was completed when James Hope and Henry Manning, Gladstone's close friends, were received into the Roman Catholic Church on Sunday, 6 April 1851, and for the time being Gladstone broke with them. The diary entry for the fourth Sunday in Lent, 30 March 1851 ran: '. . . Wrote a paper on Manning's question & gave it to him: he smote me to the ground by answering with suppressed emotion that he is now upon the *brink*: and Hope too . . .'. Then on the fifth Sunday in Lent he wrote: '. . . A day of pain!

Manning & Hope . . .'. The following day he added: '. . . Hope too is
gone. They were my two props. Their going may be to me a sign that
my work is gone with them. God give us daily light with daily bread.
One blessing I have: total freedom from doubts. These dismal events
have smitten but not shaken . . .'[38]

2

Gladstonian Liberalism in the Making

1851–1866

The ground for thinking that there was a break in Gladstone's life in 1851 is that he made a fresh beginning then. His resignation over Maynooth in 1845 is usually considered a turning-point. Although this view seems well justified, it is also true that all that happened between 1845 and 1851 had to happen before he could start afresh. His fresh start coincided with the split in the Liberal Party associated with the end of Palmerston's period as Foreign Secretary (1851) and the fall of Lord John Russell (1852). The Tory Derby-Disraeli Ministry which then followed reversed nothing that Peel, Palmerston or Russell had done. But when it ended Palmerston stood on one side and Disraeli, who had been Derby's Chancellor of the Exchequer, stood on the other as the primary political forces. When he made his fresh start, Gladstone emerged as the third force. Though he acted often with the group of Peelites, he gradually became more and more isolated, not to say unpopular, in the Commons. It turned out to be the isolation not of weakness but of strength. He had no organized or personal following, though some (and their number was increasing) began to take their cue from him. Indeed, it was to be the essence of Gladstonian Liberalism that it claimed to appeal to men's convictions and not to their party loyalty. It was a Liberal characteristic to claim to stand for what all honest and rational men would eventually come to see to be true. It was the line Gladstone later took over Home Rule for Ireland. It made him easier to caricature than to answer.

Gladstone made a fresh start in 1851 in a second way in that he began then to feel a particular liking for audiences of working men. On 14 May 1851 he attended a workers' meeting at Shadwell. He noted not only the 'very powerful speeches' by three of them, but also that all 'were delightful to see and hear: apart from the excess of their grateful feeling' towards him.[1] When Gladstone later appealed to the people, he had in his mind's eye the massed audiences of the people in the Free Trade Hall in Manchester before whom he made three speeches in October 1853, or the men he addressed at the meeting of the Federation of Mechanics' Institutes. There is no need to enlarge on the emergence of 'the labour aristocracy'. It was noticed in 1851 at the Great Exhibition and has become a commonplace of historical explanation. Palmerston's main appeal was to a different group. When he gained popular support for his foreign policy by publishing extensive Blue Books (the bulky antecedent of the White Paper) or was called to power in 1855 during the Crimean War by a movement of public opinion, his public comprised men of 'light and learning'. They were people with more leisure for reading and thinking, who also made up his audiences during his speaking tours. Palmerston, with his roots in the eighteenth century and his protection of place and patronage, was 'always quarrelling'[2] with Gladstone. Gladstone fought Palmerston as well as Disraeli in order to gain power and the lines of battle were drawn in the fifties. There is no doubt that Gladstone was out for power: power to match his ability as well as his ambition, and power which would exact its price in responsibility and unending effort. And 'populism' was to be one means of gaining it.

Finally he made a fresh start in 1851 in that he began then to mark himself out as a motive force for change. He was interested first in institutional reform, changes in the universities, Civil Service and government departments, secondly in financial reform and changes in the institutions which ran the nation's finances, and thirdly in parliamentary change. Gladstonian Liberalism stood for a forward-looking active government and strong emphasis on the individual's responsibility for his own poverty or wealth, sickness or health, employment and social mobility. Paradoxically, it was by opposing Russell that Gladstone cleared himself of a reputation for reactionary religious bigotry. Tuesday, 25 March 1851, was a major parliamentary occasion. It was the fourth night of the debate on Russell's anti-papalist, illiberal Ecclesiastical Titles Bill. Gladstone, having waited to be called for nearly five hours on the previous evening, at last, at a quarter to eleven, had his chance and he spoke against it, after considerable bookish preparation, for two and a quarter hours. He found only ninety-four others to vote with him against a majority of 438. There was no force in that majority, because the bill was an over-reaction to the Pope's use of an English place-name for a Roman Catholic diocese. Gladstone had done himself much good especially with those that had been inclined to laugh at the book of 1838 and the Maynooth resignation. His minority had lost a short-term battle but he had won the chance to look credible as a Liberal in the future.

In July 1851 Gladstone published *A Letter to the Earl of Aberdeen on the State Prosecutions of the Neapolitan Government*. He had begun this public protest against Neapolitan tyranny on 9 March after his return from the Italian journey on which in July 1849 he first read Leopardi's *Canti*. (Leopardi was a major bookish pleasure of his middle life.[3]) On the same journey he had a long conversation with one of the martyrs to the cause of Italian unity, G. Poerio, in prison in Naples, as well as much other talk and reading. He sent his letter to Aberdeen on 7 April. He began a second letter on 12 July and published it five days later.[4] In June his translation of the first two volumes of L. C. Farini, *Lo Stato di Romano, 1815–50* had been published and the third volume followed before the end of the year. A preface to the first volume made his sympathies clear. In foreign policy, Gladstone, up to now only noticed as a Peelite opponent of Palmerstonian assertiveness, had publicly and unmistakably attached himself to a forward-looking, reforming Liberalism. His personal commitment to the Italian cause was strengthened and deepened during the summer and autumn by reading the works of Mazzini and Cesare Balbo's history of Italy to 1844, not to mention less well-known works, and by correspondence with Massimo d'Azeglio. For the public he also wrote a review of the Italian edition of Farini's book.[5]

Gladstone's main work during this year was to serve on the Royal Commission for the Exhibition of 1851. Originally appointed to enquire into education for industrial design, it organized this highly profitable display of industrial products, British, colonial and foreign, in the Crystal Palace, built especially for the occasion using the railway-station technique of iron and glass.[6] Prince Albert was also a member and found a common interest with Gladstone in the progress of industrial techniques. Another colleague, Lord Granville, became a close friend and his principal coadjutor from 1868 to 1886 when he sat beside him in the Cabinet and conducted an almost daily interchange of letters with him.

Gladstone, of course, as a Peelite was a possible recruit for the Derby-Disraeli Ministry of 1852; but Derby had not persuaded him to join, though he tried. Instead his Ministry ended with a dramatic confrontration. Disraeli, who had made a provisional financial statement in April, presented his full budget in December 1852. By the fourth night of the debate the Government had every appearance of gaining a good majority. Disraeli expected to carry the division easily with his final speech. The House was crowded when he rose at twenty minutes past ten. At 1 a.m. he sat down amid tremendous applause: the unexpected then happened. Instead of an immediate division, Gladstone rose. He began quietly by correcting an error, but he passed on to rebuke Disraeli for some of his most stinging and least parliamentary language. When he continued mercilessly to dissect the financial statement of three nights ago, an unseasonable thunderstorm rattled the window panes in tune with the drama of the occasion. After 3 a.m. he sat down and the division was taken. The Government lost by nineteen votes and resigned later that day, Friday, 17 December 1852.[7]

Disraeli had said that night 'England does not love coalitions', but it was a coalition government, prepared by negotiation during the summer, which now came in. In January 1853 Lord Aberdeen as Prime Minister headed a Cabinet of Whigs (from the Commons five out of an available 270) and Peelites (from Lords and Commons four out of an available thirty). Since Gladstone succeeded Disraeli as Chancellor of the Exchequer and in April carried his budget proposals in the Cabinet against the opposition of Palmerston, the Home Secretary, and then in the House of Commons by a majority of seventy-one, the question is fairly asked what was at issue? The substance of the two budgets may be tabulated.

	Disraeli	*Gladstone*
1	*Indirect taxation:* revenue from malt tax, hop tax and tea duty all to be reduced with a loss of £3m.	Duties on a list of articles were to be abolished and reduced on an equal list of others; excise and stamp duties reduced
2	*Direct taxation,* income tax:	
(a)	its incidence was to be spread by extending it to Ireland and lowering the level at which it was payable from £150 to £100 income p.a.	The same

(b) its fairness was to be increased by distinguishing income from property paying 7*d*. in the £ and earned or salaried income paying 5*d*. in the £

The differential was not made but the prospect held out of eventual disappearance, being levied at 7*d*. for two years, 6*d*. for the next two, 3*d*. for the next three, 0*d*. in 1860

3 *Other taxation,* house tax: an existing tax, to be doubled

Other taxation, legacy duty: no more tax was to be levied on houses but the legacy duty hitherto paid on succession to personal property was to be extended to succession to land[8]

It will be seen that Disraeli's budget was the more political, the reductions of indirect taxation being targeted at particular non-urban interests. Gladstone's experience at the Board of Trade and his mastery of the tariff, however, enabled him to avoid raising the political issue of town versus country and to cast his proposals here in a way generally welcome. Disraeli's proposals on the income tax represented widely accepted views, but Gladstone, while not going against these, added the welcome innovation of a plan for seven years ahead. Under the third head, Gladstone substituted a fair extension of an existing and efficient tax for increase to a tax difficult to assess fairly. Disraeli's budget was clever. Gladstone's was one of the notable budgets of the century entitled to that description by the financial knowledge and thought behind it. Both men were meeting the need for extra expenditure on defence, neither of them offering a plan of dogmatic reform. Yet behind the coherence of Gladstone's planning lay a latent intention to switch direction from concentration on how the revenue was levied to the way in which it was spent. It remained latent till 1860.

In March 1854 the Crimean War began. In April the second of Gladstone's thirteen budgets was, therefore, provisional and completed by a supplementary one in May. To pay for the war Gladstone doubled income tax from 7*d*. to 1*s*. 2*d*., increased the duties on sugar, spirits and malt and raised a loan. He would have preferred financing the war entirely from current income but could not do so. But Sir G. Cornewall Lewis who succeeded him as Chancellor of the Exchequer in February 1855 created most of the wartime indebtedness as well as further increasing customs and excise duties.[9]

The war between Russia and Turkey began in October 1853, was joined by Britain and France in March 1854 and lasted till 1856. Gladstone was always to defend it as a just war fought to assert the interest of 'Europe' in preventing Turkey from being swallowed up by Russia. He had three grounds for such a belief. First, when Russia occupied the Turkish Danubian principalities (now Romania) she was taking hostile action against Turkey for the ninth time within a century. Second, when Turkey then opened hostilities on the Danube against the Russian occupying forces (23 October 1853), it was a nationalist[10] defiant Turkey resisting Russian demands which, because they related to the future, infringed its sovereign independence. Nicholas II demanded a convention guaranteeing Russia's rights as protector of the Orthodox Christians in the whole Turkish Empire. The original dispute between Russian and French protectors of the Holy Places in Jerusalem and Bethlehem, a tiny piece of the Empire, had been settled already six months before (22 April 1853). Third, the Treaty of London of 1841 was a European regulation for a part of the Turkish Empire (the Straits of the Bosphorus and Dardanelles) and gave good standing ground for claiming the fate of Turkey was a European concern and for resisting hints that Nicholas had made for a territorial share-out, if as a result of his demands the Turkish Empire collapsed. Unfortunately Britain had not put a stop to such hints until 1853. But after that the British ambassador to Turkey, Stratford de Redcliffe, had encouraged Turkey to resist Russia and the British and French fleets had gone to the Aegean and then to Besika Bay outside the Straits. Britain and France had been finally precipitated into alliance with Turkey (12 March 1854) by the Russian destruction of the Turkish fleet at Sinope in December 1853, though it was a perfectly legitimate operation of war. The scene of operations now moved from the Danube to the Crimean peninsula. Britain had persuaded France to exploit the command of the Black Sea which their fleets had obtained and to limit the scope of operations to capturing the forts which sheltered the Russian fleet and to destroy at Sebastopol an accessible concentration of Russian war material.[11]

War was the background to the first Gladstonian reforms. Gladstone was still member for Oxford University. The Universities Bill of 1854 was now largely drafted by him and he was responsible for putting it through the House of Commons, though as Chancellor of the Exchequer he had no departmental responsibility which made this natural. The bill was the first of his institutional reforms. Gladstone took up the recommendations of the report of a Royal Commission of

Enquiry appointed by Russell. His measure was successful because it enacted provisions which gave the universities the framework of government on a representative basis and, by enabling the alteration of charters and perpetual endowments to take place, allowed them to set their own affairs in order. It was as notable a step in increasing Gladstone's authority in the Commons as his budgets had been. Disraeli, who had begun 1853 'pugnacious and censorious', ended the session in silence and did not improve his hold on the House by what Morley called his 'high fantastic trifling' over the Universities Bill.[12] Then he made a blunder in calculation in opposing Gladstone's increase in the malt tax in the supplementary wartime budget of May 1854. Gladstone's pouncing on this and his elaborate analysis in his diary of the advantages which the blunder gave him suggests that he was bent on consolidating an ascendancy which he seemed to have won.[13]

The military operations of the war developed slowly. The victories of Alma (September), Balaclava (October) and Inkerman (November), on the way to Sebastopol, were followed by the winter-long siege of the fort. But the real tale was one of missed opportunities, disease from the first landings at Eupatoria and misery in the trenches outside Sebastopol, which the Russians did not finally abandon until September 1855. The operations were minutely watched by Gladstone[14] for they raised for him another congenial subject—administration, its efficiency and cost-effectiveness. His mind had been engaged with the subject of administrative reform since the Trevelyan-Northcote report presented in November 1853. Charles Trevelyan was a Treasury official and Sir Stafford Northcote, later Chancellor of the Exchequer, was then Gladstone's private secretary seconded from the Treasury. Gladstone's attempt to carry out the recommendations of the report (entry by competitive examination, promotion by merit as well as seniority and superannuation) resulted in an Order in Council, which he drafted, setting up the Civil Service Commission as an examining body and a bill on superannuation which he also prepared. The one was issued and the other enacted under the next Government in 1855. Gladstone's share of credit was that he shaped and planted in the official and public mind the concept of a single civil service, which could then be arranged and regulated as a whole. The idea which had prevented reform up to then was that each department had its own particular 'establishment' down to porters and 'necessary woman' which it ran in its own way.

Public indignation—fired by reports from newspaper correspondents using the new telegraph from the front—at the way the Crimean War was being run, focused on the War Office and the Duke of Newcastle at its head. In the House of Commons the outcry was led by John Roebuck, a politician of Canadian origins, who moved for an enquiry in January 1855. This Gladstone opposed on the grounds that Roebuck's intention was 'punitive' and a committee would hamper, not improve, operations and would be an unconstitutional interference with the executive. His was the best speech on the Government side. Nevertheless, Roebuck's motion was carried and the Aberdeen Government resigned. Everything in February 1855 turned on Palmerston. Clamour for him to become Prime Minister and win the war was loud. The Queen, however, acted constitutionally and sent for the leader of the Opposition, the Tory Lord Derby. Among those who refused to serve under him were the Peelites: Gladstone, Herbert and Graham. This was Derby's second overture to Gladstone—a pointer to his growing force and independence. The Queen next sent for Lord Lansdowne, leader of the Whigs, and he, too, invited Gladstone to serve under him. Gladstone refused and his refusal was decisive. He refused because Lansdowne was not enough of a 'motive force'. He later thought he had made an error because Palmerston proved to be even less of a mover for change than Lansdowne would have been.[15] Gladstone and three Peelites joined Palmerston who became Prime Minister, but they stayed only a fortnight. When Palmerston granted Roebuck his enquiry (22 February), they resigned.

During 1855, indeed until 1858, Gladstone sat on the Government side of the House but below the gangway. He continued to grow as an independent force courted by both sides. The year 1855 was to end with a social visit of Derby's son to Hawarden. The new Cabinet showed a more warlike spirit while the country adopted the war as its own. The chances of a successful conclusion were improved when Nicholas II died and the inexperienced Alexander II became Tsar. Both Gladstone and Disraeli were against the continuation of the war in 1856. Parliamentary politics were concerned with pressure for information about peace negotiations at Vienna in 1855, for administrative reform and opposition to a British guarantee of a loan to Turkey. On these topics Gladstone and Disraeli were both attacking Palmerston. They attacked from different directions and in a different tone. Disraeli was sarcastic and could make Palmerston look foolish. Gladstone deliberately distanced himself from Disraeli and was constructive, however critical. This constructive bent of mind was especially evident in the programme for future action which he drew up in February 1856. It was a pointer to the great executive statesman he was to become. Dated 16 February 1856, the memorandum was secret but commented on by his fellow Peelite, Sir James Graham. It marshalled his intentions under twenty-one headings. It is too long and too technical to reproduce. Its general tendency was to make the Chancellor of the Exchequer the single strong Finance Minister, eliminating for example the independence of the judicial account, to unify the auditing of accounts and to increase accountability to Parliament. It included the abolition of the paper duty and the further reduction of wine, malt, sugar and coffee duties.[16]

Meanwhile in Parliament he continued to speak on the same side as Disraeli. They were together in protesting against a provision in a bill on County Court judges which allowed their salaries to be fixed, within prescribed limits, *ad hominem*. 'Disraeli', wrote Gladstone, 'did good service'.[17] They were equally dissatisfied with the way of handling Russell's resolutions on education, ten days later. Privately, Gladstone thought that neither Russell nor Palmerston 'would be satisfactory as ministers with reference to the administrative work to be done' and something of his mind may have been visible since he discussed this view with his fellow Peelites.[18] But Gladstone, Aberdeen, Graham, Herbert and Cardwell though they 'communicated together habitually & confidentially' did not act as a party. They were independent individuals and individually accessible. It was clear that Derby was angling for Gladstone when an evening party given by Mrs Gladstone on 16 April was 'rather well attended by Ld Derby's friends'.[19] Indeed, Derby's third overture followed the very next day, made through a common friend, Gladstone's colleague in the representation of Oxford University, Sir William Heathcote. There were several conversations with Heathcote and consultations among the Peelites but it was all open-ended and indecisive. May to July 1856 was dominated by the Congress and then the Peace of Paris and Gladstone drew away from Derby towards Palmerston. On the war and its conclusion he agreed with Palmerston. 'It is almost the first time in the history of the world', he said in Parliament, 'that we have seen a war begun and continued with such perfect purity of motives on the part of the Powers principally concerned as in that war which has just been concluded'.[20] Yet he would distance himself from Palmerston too. In the same debate he mixed with his general approval of the Treaty of Paris a remarkably far-sighted criticism of the provision for the neutralization of the Black Sea. 'In a state of peace no doubt the arrangement would work well, but so would all systems' but if Russia again attacked Turkey, in war, 'I believe you will find that neutralization means nothing but a series of pitfalls, which, when you come to test them, you will find to be deeper than you expected.'[21] Russia repudiated the provision in 1870 (see p.64). Before the end of the year his independence of Palmerston was so marked that a fourth overture came from Lord Derby. This time it was through W. Elwin, who had succeeded Lockhart as editor of the *Quarterly Review,* for which Gladstone was then writing an article 'Prospects political and financial', which appeared in January 1857. No follow-up, however, came from Derby himself and Gladstone wrote to Aberdeen on 2 January 1857 that, 'The great Derby case has for the present at least ended in smoke'.[22]

The growth in independence and authority and the experience of being courted by both sides continued through 1857. The political year opened in fact with a harmless letter from Derby to which Gladstone replied. He and Disraeli both spoke against the Government in the debate on the Address, Gladstone for one and a quarter hours. 'I think we dealt a smart blow to the boundless extravagance of Government,' he recorded on 3 February. Derby talked with him for three hours next day. He continued concert with Derby and accompanied it by discussions with Aberdeen and the three other Peelites with whom he habitually acted. He recorded much financial work and the whole activity culminated in a tremendous attack on Cornewall Lewis's budget. Disraeli and Gladstone were speaking on the same side, though still in rivalry. Gladstone had the better basis for attack because he was pleading for the balanced kind of settlement of taxes he had made in 1853. Important for the present argument is that concert with the Tories had brought on 14 February the fifth overture from Derby; it was rejected on the 21st, after some pointed reflections, like the others.[23] Events resulting from Palmerston's browbeating policy against China roused Cobden and his group of 'pacifists' in the Commons. Their opposition was joined by the Tories and by Gladstone. He spoke for two hours, 'the finest speech in the memory of MPs then living . . . It won several votes'.[24] Cobden's motion was carried against the Government and it resigned. Gladstone's common ground with the Tories seemed plainer than ever. During the general election which followed, Gladstone recorded that he 'would not willingly run the risk of wounding Ld Derby or any friend of his',[25] nor let his Oxford University constituents think the Peelites and Liberals had coalesced.[26]

The election turned out to be a triumph for Palmerston, who remained Prime Minister. The new Parliament was confronted with the

Divorce and Matrimonial Causes Bill introduced into the House of Lords on 11 May. When it reached the Commons it occupied the House until August. Once again Gladstone and Disraeli were on the same side, however different their reasons. Gladstone was not against the legal right to dissolve a marriage, but he opposed the Bill's unequal treatment of men and women and its allowing the remarriage of a divorced man or woman in church. This time he was in a minority and the bill passed, but it had brought fresh soundings from Derby. The next successful attack upon Palmerston came when the Cobdenite Radicals carried a motion to reject Palmerston's Conspiracy to Murder Bill, introduced after an attempt to assassinate Napoleon III with an allegedly British bomb. Gladstone again spoke and voted against Palmerston. On 20 February 1858 Palmerston resigned and then Derby was engaged in forming yet another minority government. He offered Gladstone the choice of offices and said he was also ready to include the Peelite, Herbert, in his Government. Gladstone declined the same day (Sunday, 21 February). But over the use of the Indian army, as over Scottish education, he was only able to gain his objectives by speaking with the Tories, and in May Disraeli in a curious incident offered to give up the lead of the House of Commons to the Peelite, Graham, if Gladstone would join the Government. As late as July 1858 Derby still hoped for Gladstone's 'alliance'. On important and conspicuous occasions on 31 March (see p.46) and 10 June 1859, Gladstone still voted with the Tories. Yet when Derby's Government fell three days later Gladstone joined Palmerston's last Government as Chancellor of the Exchequer (13 June). The Tory of 1833 had thus become a Liberal. Gladstone had changed sides but he was never called a renegade. His presence in the Liberal Governments of 1859 to 1866 seemed to have resulted from persons and processes clarifying round him while he himself stood still, gradually consolidating his position as a third, if isolated, force. Derby never seems to have thought that he could only have Gladstone if he took in all five Peelites. It was Gladstone he wanted and 'alliance' was not an inappropriate word. Gladstone's force lay in his power to change men's minds and to carry their votes and it was worth having by itself.

Gladstone was articulate − on paper as well as in speech − about his reasons for declining Derby's openings and they reveal the man he was. One reason was Disraeli. In a memorandum of 14 February 1857 Gladstone wrote that he had told Derby that 'from motives which I could neither describe nor conquer I was quite unable to enter into any squabble or competition with him [Disraeli] for the possession of a post

of prominence'.[27] The remark related only to the narrow subject of
competition in leading the attack on Cornewall Lewis's budget, but it
is consistent with a wider interpretation. It was as if Gladstone rejected
petty rivalry for the leadership of the Tory parliamentary party because
he preferred a greater battle — the battle before the country's electorate
between himself, leader of one party, and Disraeli, leader of the other.
Gladstone was enormously ambitious. He wanted power commensurate
with his abilities, and would be frustrated without it. Moreover, only
under Palmerston could he carry out the programme he had sketched
out in February 1856, for he knew from 1853 that on finance he could
argue Palmerston to a standstill. Nominally 'under' the premier, he
would actually be equal. And he would be exercising strength precisely,
as their budgets had shown, where Disraeli was weakest. The other
reason for declining Derby's several overtures is indicated in the
memorandum of the conversation of 6 March 1857 with Derby.
Gladstone criticized in carefully chosen words Derby's political behaviour. The drift of his criticism was Derby's indifference to opinion
outside Parliament. Gladstone himself was well known in Scotland, in
Wales as a holidaymaker, in industrial Lancashire and Staffordshire and
the North East, in rural Cheshire and in southern counties as well as in
London. From 1851 onwards he was increasingly concerned with
popular politics. The speeches of 1851 and 1853 have been mentioned;
next he was acutely aware of the force of opinion that brought
Palmerston to power in 1854–55 ('the world is drunk about a
P[almerston] Government'[28]); over Palmerston's foreign policy he had
recently shown his sympathies with Cobden and Bright and he was fully
aware how 'populist' they were. His series of speeches to popular
audiences in the sixties is referred to later in this chapter. Derby's
conservatism — Peelite conservatism was 'dead', he had noted on 12
May 1857 — was too exclusively parliamentary ever fully to have
engaged Gladstone.

   In November 1858 Gladstone began a mission to the Ionian Islands
undertaken at the invitation of the Derby Government. There was a
nationalist movement in the Islands for annexation to Greece and
freedom from the British protectorate which had existed from 1815. The
mission touched topics of absorbing interest to Gladstone. First,
nationality: from the time of his taking up the movement for Italian
freedom and unification in 1851 this interest had grown by watching the
movement for Romanian unification after the Peace of Paris had
provided in 1856, in somewhat ambiguous terms which a further

conference in Paris had been forced to clarify, for the unity and independence from Turkey of the Romanian Principalities. On his way back from his mission in the spring of 1859, and just before the war of Sardinia and France against Austria which enabled Cavour to begin to make the Italian kingdom, Gladstone had an hour's conversation with Cavour. Second, the Eastern Question: Gladstone was still ready to justify the defence of Turkey against Russia as a European interest, however clearly he dissociated himself from the mismanagement of the Crimean War. He read some dozen works on the Ottoman Empire and its peoples during 1855–68. He recommended in his report on his mission, not that the islanders' national aspirations should be satisfied, but that nationality should yield before the more important interests of the Kingdom of Greece and the strategic interests of Britain until such time as the political reconstruction of the whole of south-eastern Europe could be attempted. That was 'the very great question' of which the small Ionian question was 'the narrow corner'.[29] Gladstone recommended constitutional reform and was indeed commissioned to carry it out before he came home. Thus Britain kept the Protectorate until 28 May 1864, when the islands were at last annexed to Greece. Third, Homer: all the places he visited had some association with Homer or later Greek history. Gladstone had filled the long intermissions from parliamentary duties in November 1846 to September 1847 (when domestic pressures stopped study) and 1855 to 1858 with hard work on Homer, of which *Studies of Homer and the Homeric Age* in three volumes of respectable scholarship was the not inconsiderable outcome.

The preparation for publication filled a personal need. The sudden end of brain work under high pressure in 1846 and 1855 would have been unbearable without something else for the brain to work at. On both occasions he returned with intense delight to his schoolboy and young man's reading of *Iliad* and *Odyssey*. Writing followed reading for the system-making urge of his mind was intolerable until released on paper. Publication followed writing, also for a personal reason: 'the remote idea of the fruits of study, as intended in some way to reach others' was a remedy to the selfishness of enjoyment.[30] Yet the publication in 1858 was premature, partly because of the speculative theories of volume two which he did not fully repeat in later works. Essentially these rest upon a distinction between what he called Homer's 'traditive' Gods and his 'invented' Gods. He argues for an original universal revelation (using the book of Genesis as evidence) of one God, even of one God in three persons, antedating all history. This revelation by Homer's time had been corrupted. Corruption had taken the form of disintegration: of making one into many. But a tradition survived. 'Traditive' is especially applied to Zeus, Apollo and Athene. He comes near to saying, but never actually says, that Apollo was a reflection of the idea of Christ the Redeemer. This bald statement reduces to near nonsense what is in fact subtle and speculative and, in being rooted in the Homeric and other texts, scholarly. In sensing generally the religious feeling of Homer, Gladstone finds sympathy among modern scholars. In particularizing he becomes unacceptable.

The virtue of the *Studies* lies in volumes one and three. But even volume one, which attempts to disentangle from Homer's use of such terms as Danaan, Achaian and Argive the successive movements of peoples into the Greek peninsula and coast of Asia Minor, was premature. Gladstone was later to modify its conclusions to incorporate the results of nineteenth-century archaeology. The lasting value of both volumes one and three is in their reflection of the kind of mind he brought to his political career. The questions broached in volume one were prompted by Gladstone's belief that nationality was the supreme political force of the age. His method is that of someone determined to convince and conclusions which begin as possibilities easily become premises for new arguments. When he makes the surprising assertion that Homer's purpose '. . . was to unite more closely the elements of the [Greek] nation, and not to record that they had once been separate',[31] he is telling us how important the idea of nationality was to him as statesman rather than the truth about Homer. Gladstone was always ready to trace back liberal ideas to Ancient Greece. In volume three he plainly stated that they began in Homeric Greece and can be seen in their earliest form in the *Iliad* and *Odyssey* where 'the strength and simplicity' of social relations was remarkable and the characters in the poems were pervaded by an 'intense political spirit'.[32] He developed his meaning by showing that alongside the characteristic features of a patriarchical society 'we find the full, constant and effective use, of two great instruments of [popular] government . . . namely publicity and persuasion'.[33] The discussion is cast towards institutions and constitutions. It comes to life only when Gladstone writes from his own experience and the reader can catch the sound of discussion or of debate in the House of Commons. He noticed how each speech in the *Iliad* answered another. He characterized each speaker's style and when he wrote of Thersites' speech — 'But if we regard it, as every speech should be regarded, with reference to some paramount purpose, it is really senseless and inconsequent'[34] – he betrayed something about his own speaking methods. Precautions he himself effectively took are indicated when he remarks on the chief cause of a speech's failure being that the speaker's own vanity blocked his vision. Gladstone on the Homeric art of persuasion was Gladstone on his own oratory.

This is not to disparage his literary observation. What he said on Homer's notion of colour, his epithets and his similes or attitude to number is of lasting interest. His literary instinct was sound when it led him to avoid the controversy about Homer's single or multiple identity in order not to obscure the literary value of what has come down to us in the *Iliad* and the *Odyssey* taken together. Yet the two dominant interests of his life, political power and religion, are never far away. For example, in discussing the 'plot' of the *Iliad* he attributes to Achilles a desire for retributive justice and uses this desire to explain Achilles' rejection of Agamemnon's offer of reparation.[35] This is out of key with Homer's ideas and Gladstone has no justification for it except his own perennial concern with justice, perhaps the bridge which bound his political, religious and, indeed, literary life together.

The Ionian mission renewed in Gladstone the contentment that always came with achievement. But the happiness of the forward-looking young man of the thirties and forties had already been renewed at Hawarden in the summer. August 1858 was a month of happy family activity. He was reading Ariosto with Willie and Agnes, and Horace with Stephy. 'We have now', he records, 'ordinarily a family song or dance after dinner.'[36] Woodcutting went on in the afternoon of most days. The people's William, tree-felling axe in hand, the popular image of the seventies and eighties, was taking shape in his renewal of contact with large working-class audiences that he had first made in 1851. On 5 November 1860 at Chester, after a review of the Volunteers, he made a speech to 'a crowded meeting at the Music Hall' and was received with 'tremendous cheering'.[37] It was an awkward occasion cleverly handled, for he cried up the Volunteer movement while decrying the current alarm about war with France. On 10 October 1861, after opening the Liverpool School of Science, he addressed 'a Mass Meeting at St George's Hall' on the promotion of science, while feeling something of 'a Charlatan'.[38] Next year, 23 April 1862, he addressed a meeting of the Lancashire and Cheshire Mechanics' Institutes in the Free Trade Hall in Manchester, 'crowded with a most cordial auditory'.[39] In the autumn something like the popular speaking tours of 1879–80 took place on a smaller scale and continued intermittently until 1864. The Civil War in America and the consequent cotton famine in Lancashire gave him the stuff of his oratory. On 7 October 1862 after touring the sights of Newcastle in the afternoon, when a photographer 'laid hands' on him, he attended 'a crowded & enthusiastic dinner of near 500'. The occasion became notorious since in his long oration he referred to the Confederate leader, Jefferson Davis, as having 'made a nation': this led to Gladstone's reputation of bias towards the South. During the next two days on Tyneside he went on a river expedition through 'great multitudes of people' with 'as many speeches as hours', inspected docks and harbour works and addressed meetings at Darlington, Sunderland and Middlesborough. From Hawarden, where he retreated, he visited Wrexham for the opening of the Connah's Quay railway. It was a popular occasion with a 'very warm' reception and a speech on railways. On 27 December he spoke at Chester on the cotton famine and Lancashire distress 'to a very crowded meeting'. The next year, 1863, saw his address to the workmen of the Wedgwood factory, subsequently published. In October 1864 came meetings at Bolton and Manchester. At Bolton after a public reception at the railway station there was 'a dense assembly' in the Temperance Hall and he was 'much struck with the people'. At Manchester he estimated 3,000 present at the Exchange meeting and 6,000 at the next meeting in the Free Trade Hall. It was 'impossible not to love the people from whom such manifestations come, as met me in every quarter'.[40]

His power to draw the crowds and to hold their minds was wonderful. That he could hold Scots and Welshmen, cockneys and Liverpudlians, Geordies and West Country men and women may have owed something to their all being accustomed in church and chapel to the hour-long sermon and the language of the Bible, if not the Book of Common Prayer. It was, none the less, remarkable. The magic cannot be recaptured from the verbatim reports of long orations in arid columns of newspaper small print. Yet these do suggest possible explanations. First, he made no concessions in thought or language. He attracted, therefore, the hero-worship of the thinking yet excluded people — people excluded, that is, from schools and universities and other homes of thought. There were many such people in the days of *The Popular Educator* (published in monthly parts) and self-improvement and when a working life began with or before adolescence. Second, behind all his arguments and leading on to the detail and illustration were broad considerations of humanity and justice. A man whose friends ranged from Dr Döllinger of Munich and Lord Acton to John Morley, from

Catholics to free-thinkers; whose women intimates were successively the Duchess of Sutherland and the courtesan Laura Thistlethwayte; who was a welcome guest at both Hatfield (Lord Salisbury, later Prime Minister) and Walmer (Lord Granville) must have had a more than usual understanding of common human emotions and a universal sympathy. Third, he had a most musical voice, a good ear, a fiery eye and a commanding presence (however crumpled his clothes). That Hawarden became a place of pilgrimage attests to a faith quite outside the normal experience of political Britain. It may, indeed, in the last Home Rule phase of his life have betrayed him into a rigidity out of keeping with the flexibility of his early and middle life and of his first ministry. But that commitment in itself raised hero-worship.

In the general election of 1865, when he stood not for Oxford University but for South West Lancashire, he spoke of 'the daily penny press [his own abolition of the paper duty in 1861 explained that low price] that finds its way into the house of the working man . . . keeps him well-informed without the least disparagement of other classes, upon public affairs . . . making him feel that he has become in a new sense a citizen of his country'. Gladstone's 'astute use of the press' began from this basis. It was seen especially in his relations with the *Daily Telegraph,* a penny paper with a daily circulation exceeding that of *The Times.* He passed exact and detailed information to one of its reporters, T.L. Hunt, at the end of the Palmerston Government in 1865, and after that was in constant touch with Levy Lawson, whose family owned it. Much of the provincial press took its Westminster news from the *Daily Telegraph* and it was the *Daily Telegraph* which created the image of the People's William.[41]

In June 1859 Gladstone resumed his 'old office' under Palmerston with an air of inevitability. The Liberal Party was reunited and offered Gladstone the opportunity of joining a strong government, where he would be in a position to get things done. He was strong enough in himself at least to move forward on the programme of 1856 (see p.30) even if Palmerston was no motive force. He served as Chancellor of the Exchequer from June 1859 to July 1866. Not one of his successors held that office for the period of seven consecutive years until Hicks Beach from 1895 to 1902, and then Lloyd George, 1908–15. Gladstone was unique in taking office with a programme of measures he intended to carry through. He left the day-to-day work to the financial secretary to the Treasury and to the civil servants. He found 'Treasury business much heavier', as he wrote to Catherine, 'than when I was last in office.

If I were willing to let money flow very freely it might be made easy enough: but at every point I have the wearisome business of offering resistance'.[42] The only matters of detail where he intruded related to the negotation of contracts: one over the so-called Galway packet for communication with North America; the other for the Red Sea Telegraph.[43] His interest was in securing the most economical arrangements.

His main business was 'the measured preparation' of the annual budget, usually begun at Hawarden in December. The estimates provided by the different spending departments, chiefly the Admiralty and War Office, gave him a basis and he would call on the Board of Inland Revenue or the National Debt Commissioners to provide him with information as and when he needed it. Gladstone's chief aim of strengthening Treasury control over the departments and of turning the Chancellor of the Exchequer into a powerful independent Finance Minister was thus achieved. Treasury control was secured through the machinery of the estimates which came to it and were co-ordinated, even questioned, by it, before January, and through relieving the Exchequer of all functions except receiving the revenue and exercising a first check on accounting. Gladstone did not consult his Cabinet colleagues until the process of preparing his proposals was finished. He then brought them to the Cabinet and proceeded to argue for their acceptance with his usual masterful elaboration, complete exactitude and an apparently inexhaustible wealth of information. It would have taken another Chancellor of the Exchequer to defeat him. He took his proposals through a hostile Cabinet successfully in 1860 and 1861, and later devised ways of evading Palmerston's opposition.[44] But estimates were 'settled at dagger's point' in 1865 as in 1860.

The proposals were next taken to the Commons and carried by Palmerston's healthy majority. They were directed to three objects. First, he aimed at producing a balanced version of the taxation system towards which he had made considerable progress in 1853. In July 1859 he presented a provisional budget temporarily raising income tax to meet a deficit of £5m.[45] In 1860 he lowered wine, brandy and silk duties, renewed the tea and sugar duties for one year and then in 1861 abolished them together with the paper duty. The attempts to abolish the paper duties in 1860 provoked a major row with the House of Lords and a constitutional innovation which prevented it from interfering with the abolition in 1861. But he was not able to abolish the income tax because of the second object he had to achieve. This was to meet the necessary demands of regular expenditure. In 1861–65 interest on the National Debt accounted for 37.7 per cent of expenditure, defence 39.4 per cent, other costs of government 15.4 per cent and the costs of revenue collection and other small charges 7.5 per cent. Gladstone made no attempt to reduce the charge of the National Debt, since he saw that it had its political and economic advantages. He believed that if retrenchment was to be achieved he must cut defence expenditure. Economy and retrenchment became a chief part of the business of meeting regular expenditure but it proved impossible to achieve by cutting defence costs. In the last resort defence ministers, challenged over their estimates by the Treasury, came to the Cabinet. Gladstone during this period never provoked an argument over estimates that might have split the Cabinet: so he yielded. The third object at which he aimed his proposals was provision for extraordinary expenditure on imperial ventures or demonstrations demanded by foreign policy. In this period the cost of the erection of forts on the south coast to meet an alleged danger from France in 1860 had to be met. Gladstone, rather than increase income tax from its 1s. 1d. in the £, found an alternative in the Cobden commercial treaty with France.

Gladstone always maintained that the treaty was not a commercial treaty, strictly speaking.[46] Such treaties, in the sense of tariff bargains between two countries, were betrayals of the free trade economy. The treaty provided for a simultaneous change of tariffs independently by Britain and France and equally applicable to all their other trading partners. It was negotiated as a bargain by Cobden, in his private capacity, with Napoleon III, who in the face of French protests argued that he must have 'concessions' of British duties on French wine, brandy and silk in return for relaxing the French duties on British coal, iron and manufactured goods. But it had orginated from a speech of Bright in the House of Commons protesting against the war scare with France and asking why could Britain not approach the Emperor instead of arming against him. Cobden and the French economist, M. Chevalier, had taken this up. Cobden had written to Gladstone, who had invited him to Hawarden, and the overture to France had taken shape 'during several hours walk and talk' with him on 12 and again 13 September 1859. Gladstone kept in close touch with the negotiations which followed in Paris, and Cobden on 21 December was able to use Gladstone's preparation of his budget as a means of hurrying up the reluctant French. On 11 January 1860 a 'conclave' of Cabinet ministers and Treasury officials put matters on a formal footing, Cobden received official instructions drafted by Gladstone and a draft treaty while Lord Cowley, the ambassador, was put in formal charge. On 23 January the Cobden Treaty was signed. Gladstone's speech on 10 February described the remissions of duty on wine, brandy and spirits which Britain would make and the contents of the treaty. Henceforward the remnants of British wine and spirit duties were recognized as for revenue only. In Gladstone's view it was a real alternative to Palmerston's foreign policy and justified reductions in the defence estimates which he did not get. He recorded: '31 Jan. Cabinet 1–4½ very stiff. I carried my remissions but the Depts carried their great estimates'.[47]

In addition to making the Chancellor of the Exchequer a powerful Finance Minister in the Cabinet, Gladstone was determined to increase the accountability of the financial administration to the House of Commons. This suited his legalist turn of mind but it also was a way of saving unnecessary expenditure. On 9 April 1861 he moved that a select committee be appointed for the examination from year to year of the audited accounts of the public expenditure. This was carried and the Public Accounts Committee was duly set up, its appointment at the beginning of each session being made a Standing Order of the House. In 1866 at the very end of his period at the Exchequer he was responsible for the enactment of the Exchequer and Audit Act which consolidated the Exchequer with the Audit Department. It also provided for the auditing of all expenditure of public money (whether up to then unaudited, or else audited by the Treasury or by the Exchequer) by one authority and set up a single Audit Board to do it. Gladstone was less successful in reforming the relationship of the Treasury to the Bank of England. His plan to revise the Bank Charter Act of 1844 was not even published and his Country Banks Note Issue Bill had to be withdrawn. All this had been within the programme of 1856. Two acts for which he was responsible went beyond it. They were in line with his populist attitude of these years. On 8 February 1861 Gladstone carried a resolution in the Commons 'to charge on the Consolidated Fund any deficiency in the sums which may be held on account of Post Office Savings Banks to meet the lawful demands of depositors in such banks in the event of their being founded'. They were duly founded by an Act of 1863. Then in 1864 he put through an act to enable 'the industrial classes', or small investors, to buy annuities.[48]

One of the reasons which Gladstone gave to friends, such as Acton, for joining Palmerston was the Italian question.[49] Derek Beales once argued that Italian liberty provided the general principle that always seemed necessary to Gladstone to make him act on the practical reasons which were already indicating a particular course to him.[50] Indeed, Palmerston, Russell and Gladstone came to form an Italian trio within the Cabinet. The rest of the Cabinet, whom Russell once referred to as his thirteen opponents,[51] were both more cautious and less interested than these three. Russell as Foreign Secretary nominally shaped policy towards events in Italy after Villafranca had ended the Franco-Austrian War and provided for the extension of Piedmont to the borders of Venice by the absorption of Lombardy. It provided also for restoration to the Duchies of Tuscany and Modena of their former Dukes and of papal rule to the Romagna and the end there of Piedmontese provisional governments. In fact, these restorations proved to be impossible and were not provided for in the final Peace of Zurich. Russell's moves concerned various possibilities of holding France back if Napoleon III should attempt to force these restorations. To decide policy towards France became even more important when it annexed Savoy in supposed compensation for Piedmont's further absorptions, that is of Tuscany, Parma and Modena in 1860. Finally, when Garibaldi invaded Sicily and Naples in May 1860 and achieved their union with Piedmont too, there was the possibility of joining with France to preserve some part of the South Italian *status quo*. In all this Russell showed himself a dogmatic supporter of Italian constitutionalism, but too much given to fits and starts to be the prime designer of policy.

Palmerston was the dominant member of the trio. His initiative in building up British strength against France has already been mentioned. If he sometimes supported Gladstone or Russell in proposals for co-operation or even alliance with France, he did so on purpose to control France: he continued to distrust Napoleon III and suspected him of aggrandizement. Secondly, Palmerston ensured that Britain was never in fact committed to active intervention in Italy, though he might encourage Russell in using expressions which indicated that intervention was possible. Palmerston mistrusted the aggrandizement of Piedmont as much as he did that of France, but was too much of a realist to oppose it. Thirdly, he considered the Italian question from the standpoint of the European balance and European stability, but like Russell (though unlike Gladstone) thought Europe was not integrated enough to count as a real factor in the situation.

Gladstone's position was unique since his primary interest was in the reform of the papal government. Of the two 'great objects of desire' which he noted on 30 June, one, 'the cessation of the direct dominion of Austria in Italy', had been achieved so far as it could then be, at Villafranca. The second, 'an essential change in the position of the Popedom with reference to its temporal prerogatives', then became paramount. He did not believe that the Italians by themselves were strong enough to relieve the Pope of his temporal power and knew he would concede nothing of himself. France was unreliable. He was afraid Italy might be left 'with its great central volcano'. 'If on the other hand', he wrote, '*Europe* undertakes and achieves the settlement of the question, it will be settled on better terms for both Pope and people. The Pope will then have under European guarantee, independence, security, dignity, and wealth: and his people will have some Government, established in order, and not in chaos.'[52] In October when there was just a possibility that a European Congress might meet to confirm the terms reached at Zurich, he recorded: 'Cabinet 1½–4½. We now lean (as I always did) to Congress'. By January 1860 he was denouncing the high language of Roman Catholics about perpetuating the temporal power of the papacy as constituting 'something of a challenge to all Governments as such'.[53]

Secondly, Gladstone did not share Palmerston's obsession with French aggrandizement. In so far as the Italian question was a French question it was one of how to work on France by means of those common interests with Britain which had been affirmed in the Cobden Treaty. Gladstone was ready for joint action with France and Sardinia to ensure the peaceful settlement of central Italy and was not afraid that this need mean any military commitment.[54] The ultimate outcome was very different. It was a dispute with Palmerston who answered the French annexation of Nice and Savoy with the fortifications bill to grant money for fortifying the south coast against France. This Gladstone opposed for two months, though on 21 July he gave in at last. On 2 June his 'resignation' had been '*all but*' decided during the dispute.[55]

It was in the next year, 1861, that Gladstone's relations with the Queen lost Prince Albert's influence. Shared interests with him (see p. 25), and the Queen's liking for Mrs Gladstone and kindness to the Gladstone children, had given Gladstone a good standing at court, but neither Prince nor Queen found him any support in their objections to Russell's and Palmerston's Italian and German policy in 1859–60. Then, when in December 1861 Prince Albert died, the Queen looked to Gladstone, as a notably religious man, for understanding and sympathy. She was disappointed. At his first audience there was a long conversation in which he awkwardly and pedantically left it to her to take the initiative even on this occasion. He offered nothing. In a conversation lasting nearly an hour his sympathy and support were given only in reply to her somewhat commonplace remarks and could not have seemed to her to draw on the special religious resources she had ascribed to him.[56] He continued to be kindly received at Balmoral, Osborne or Windsor, while his eldest son was later chosen as companion to one of the Queen's sons on a continental journey. Yet she felt herself overpowered by him. Another four years and Gladstone, with his usual devastating precision, recorded: 'She looked extremely well and was kind: but in all her conversations with me she is evidently hemmed in, stops at a certain point, & keeps back the thought which occurs'.[57] Then in 1866, when he became leader of the House, with the duty of reporting the events of each sitting, the solemnity of his manner of writing reinforced her fear of being put in the wrong by him. Disraeli when in office in 1866–68 exploited his opportunity. The Queen by December 1868 was resenting Gladstone's pressure to open Parliament and perform her full range of public duties despite her mourning. After 1874–80, her experience of Disraeli's wit and warmth and her sympathy with his imperialism caused confidence in Gladstone to be impossible.

In 1861 two roads were leading Gladstone towards a fresh instalment of parliamentary reform. One was financial. In his budget speech of 1861 Gladstone argued that free trade had so stimulated the economy that the country could afford high taxation, but high taxation would prove a drag on the economy in the long term. The only way to bring it down was to cut expenditure. Only the electorate could bring about real retrenchment. To widen it to include lower-paid men was to widen the demand for retrenchment. He believed there was some correlation between those who earned £100 p.a. and paid tax and those who deserved the vote. The second road was 'populist': Gladstone's increasing familiarity with massed audiences had bred in him a respect for their political commonsense. This had been much increased by the behaviour of the Lancashire cotton workers when the American Civil War, by bringing the supply of raw cotton from the South to a standstill, put them out of work. The relief works he organized for them in Hawarden Park and their behaviour there had brought them and their good sense daily under his eye.

By the mid-sixties, however, the question of parliamentary reform had acquired a momentum of its own. Russell had written a memorandum for the Cabinet already in 1851 (12 August) outlining a scheme, and in 1852 sketched a prospective bill to the Commons. Under the Aberdeen coalition Russell gained the appointment of a Cabinet committee to frame a bill. Gladstone described the Cabinet as discussing franchise reform 'largely—amicably and satisfactorily—on the whole' as if his own opinion was still unfixed.[58] Early in 1854 Russell brought in a bill. Palmerston and others resigned rather than accept it. Russell withdrew it and they returned. Silence now fell on the question. When next we hear of it (1858) Disraeli had taken it up and John Bright and the Radicals were campaigning in the country and rousing enthusiasm in Birmingham, Manchester and Glasgow. Gladstone had by this date got so far as to believe that 'no Government could now stand which blinked the question'.[59] The Derby-Disraeli Government of 1858–59 did not blink the question but introduced a bill early in 1859. Lord John Russell then moved a resolution favouring reform, but not that particular version of it. On 29 March Gladstone spoke against Russell's resolution, defending the 'small boroughs' that Russell wished to suppress and claiming that they were the nurseries of statesmen.[60] He was right historically, but his meaning for the future was nevertheless that he wanted reform. Though on 31 March he voted against Russell, his juncture with Palmerston a few months later was caused among other things by the wish to co-operate in settling the franchise question.

In 1860 Russell introduced yet another bill. It failed, but may have played a part in fixing Gladstone's mind on the economic argument for widening the franchise in 1861. On 11 May 1864 he made a famous declaration, prompted by Edward Baines's motion for parliamentary reform. It held out to the Radicals the leadership of a man who could bring over moderate opinion (that is, the Whigs) and perhaps even conciliate some Tories on the basis of 'settling' the question and forestalling a slide towards universal suffrage. He himself was surprised at 'some sensation' caused by it.[61] By this declaration also, he put the matter on the plane of general principle: 'Every man who is not presumably incapacitated by some consideration of personal unfitness or of political danger, is morally entitled to come within the pale of the constitution'. Gladstone was again applying his doctrines of adaptation and approximation (see p. 11), answering the call of empiricism as well as that of idealism. Palmerston protested that a government's duty was to calm agitation, not to yield to it, and the question slept again.

The general election of 1865, while giving Palmerston his usual majority of seventy or so, also increased the Radicals' representation and added to their number John Stuart Mill, Henry Fawcett, G.O. Trevelyan, Thomas Hughes, Duncan McLaren and other 'intellectuals'. It brought in an unusual number of new MPs. Next, Russell (now Earl Russell) again became Prime Minster after Palmerston had died on 18 October and a further attempt at reform inevitably followed. Under Radical pressure he abandoned the Commission of Enquiry, which he would at this stage have preferred, and on 10 December 1865 announced the principles of a prospective bill, leaving Gladstone to draft it and settle the details. However, three other things had happened by this date: first, a party of dissident Liberals led by Robert Lowe and Lord Elcho had emerged as opponents of all reform (the 'Adullamites'); second, after Disraeli's adoption of parliamentary reform in 1858–59 the subject had been caught up in the ruthless contest between him and Gladstone; third and most important, the several attempts and the successive debates had revealed the extreme difficulty of discovering, by any statistics that could be found, the effects of adopting a rating or a rental valuation to fix the property qualification for voting. Statistics were either unobtainable or unreliable. Rating arrangements varied from locality to locality. It was impossible to know how many new voters of the old kind one would admit by whatever level one adopted; nor how many voters of a new kind since the line between the artisan who 'deserved' the vote and labouring poor who did not was indeterminate. Nevertheless Gladstone had behind him the work of more than one Cabinet committee, much statistical and impressionistic information and an obstinate will to settle the question.

In March he brought forward a bill to widen the franchise without a rearrangement of constituencies because as Chancellor of the Exchequer, busy with his budget, he had neither time nor the mental strength to prepare one. The Cabinet had shifted from a rental to a rating qualification and back to a rental one as varying information came in. The bill, finally settled on 8 March, fixed on a £7 rental qualification in the boroughs, and made minimal changes in the counties. But he was working on the papers to the last minute, so that when on the night of 12 March he rose to ask leave to introduce the Representation of the People Bill, he was without his usual confidence, complaining of a 'stuffed' head. Only 'God's help' saw him through.[62] He justified the terms of the bill as an attempt to preserve the *status quo,* adapting the voting qualifications to keep the electorate as it was by continuing to exclude the mass of the illiterate or 'improvident'. The honours of the debate went to the opposition led by Robert Lowe, Lord Elcho and the other 'Adullamites'. Lowe argued that there was no need to lower the voting qualification because economic expansion and rising wages were enabling all those who deserved the vote to earn it at the existing qualification. During the Easter recess Gladstone spoke at Liverpool on behalf of the bill.[63] This was an indication of the way his provincial standing and his favour with the Radicals was being increased at this time. It was, however, an unprecedented move for a Cabinet minister to plead for a government bill outside Parliament when it was still under consideration there. He had asked and gained Cabinet permission to do so.

In the second reading debates Disraeli played the main part in the Opposition: the duel between the two men was never so sharp. Gladstone refused to be drawn into the statistical bog and used arguments of broad humanity. He spoke of the working men as human beings of the same stuff as his parliamentary colleagues. He accepted the amendment of Lord Grosvenor (acting for the 'Adullamites') insisting on a simultaneous rearrangement of constituencies, but the Opposition still pressed the Grosvenor amendment to a division. It provoked Gladstone's finest speech. This began with a rebuke to Disraeli, whom he followed, for 'skulking under the shelter of the meaningless amendment of the Noble Lord' and taunted him with not daring to tell the nation what he really thought. It ended with the peroration 'You may bury the Bill that we have introduced but [you] . . . cannot fight against the future . . . Time is on our side. The great social forces which move onward in their might and majesty are against you.' The Government, nevertheless, won by only five votes. Moreover, Gladstone, who after the defeat of the amendment wished to hold out against a constituencies bill, was overruled by the Cabinet.[64] This bill, then botched together, was not drafted by him. In the committee stage the franchise and constituencies bills were combined into a single bill under Opposition pressure and the Government were assailed with some major amendments. Gladstone complained to Russell of the intolerable burden. He 'was much worn by toothache and slept little'.[65] But the work went inexorably on until at the end of June the Government was defeated. The wear and tear of discussion in Cabinet and acrimony of debate in the House had since January turned not only on reform but also on compensation to farmers for the devastation of the Cattle Plague, the dismissal of Governor Eyre for over-reacting to the Jamaica riots, the financial crisis that followed the failure of the banking house of Overend and Gurney, and now in June the continental situation as the Austro-Prussian War began. Russell was worn out, could not rally a following that he had long ago failed to lead, and was ready to dissolve. Gladstone, Argyll and Milner Gibson supported him. They were overruled. 'Cabinet 3–5. Decided to resign: not without difference and in the teeth of the Queen.'[66] Gladstone believed that it was the more constitutional and honourable course to appeal to the country in the hope of being re-elected and to reintroduce the bill and carry it with the larger majority he hoped would result and settle the question once and for all. The Queen appealed to Russell to stay on in view of the continental situation. The arguments ended in the Queen's sending for Derby who formed an administration which lasted, with a change to Disraeli as Prime Minister, until 1868. The session ended with Gladstone on the Opposition bench where he had last sat fifteen years ago.

The reform question was now half settled by the act passed by Disraeli in August 1867. This qualified for the vote in the boroughs all male inhabitants of houses whether as owners or occupiers (household suffrage), male lodgers in lodgings of £10 yearly value, and, in the counties, all males who possessed land, by whatever tenure, of a clear annual value of £5 or more or who were the occupiers, whether as owners or tenants, of property of the rateable value of £12 or more. The rearrangement of constituencies and reform acts for Scotland and Ireland did not follow until 1868. The Representation of the People Bill originally introduced by Disraeli on 18 March 1867 was a far less radical measure than the eventual Act. The bill was reduced to its final form by Disraeli's acceptance of amendments during its passage. The process of its change is notorious for Disraeli's readiness to accept any amendment except the ones originating with Gladstone. Yet it was Gladstone who, from the time he followed Disraeli immediately after his speech introducing the bill, took the lead in pulling it to pieces and pointing out the statistical flaws on which it was based. 'He intended to turn the bill inside out by amending every clause but the first two.'[67] But Gladstone was faced with the 'tea-room' revolt by a group of fifty-two Radicals and on 12 April found himself and his supporters in a minority of 289 to 310: 'A smash perhaps without example . . .'[68] Nevertheless his purpose was pretty well achieved by a combination of craft and patience.

In July 1867 when the excitements of the session and struggle with Disraeli were over Gladstone returned to Homer under much the same need as the abrupt relaxation of tension has created in 1847 or 1855.

'Ruminated on proceeding about Homer' is associated by the editor of
the diaries with a revision of the *Studies* of 1858.[69] It was not until the
spring of 1869 that the revision in one volume, which is what *Juventus
Mundi* essentially is, was published. From September 1867 until
February 1869 one can follow the regular 'little morsels' or longer daily
pieces of time given either to *Juventus Mundi* or to the unpublished
Thesaurus Homericus. In January 1868 he had published a review of
Ernest Renan, *Mission de Phénicie,* (in three volumes, 1864–7) – he
had already read Renan's *Vie de Jésus*.[70] He is much more soundly
informed about Phoenicia in the *Juventus* than he showed himself in the
Studies, where some of what he wrote had been mere speculation. In
the *Juventus* there is the same emphasis on nationality, but it is more
neatly handled. Gladstone still asserts that Homer was 'Intensely
national in feeling'[71] and he repeats the sentence already quoted (p. 36)
about Homer's purpose being to unite the elements of the Greek nation
rather than to record that they had once been separate. Chapter VII,
which begins his summary and revision of the sections of the *Studies* on
religion, opens 'Homer was the maker not only of Poems; but also, in
a degree never equalled by any other poet, 1. of a language; 2. of a
nation; 3. of a religion'.[72] He has, however, jettisoned the distinction
between 'traditive' and 'invented' Gods as the basis of the argument for
Homeric religion being a corrupted version of an original universal
revelation. Instead, he now sees that 'Homer, from living in the midst
of an intermixture and fusion of bloods continually proceeding in
Greece, acquired a vast command of materials, and by his skilful use of
them exercised an immense influence in the construction of the Greek
religion',[73] though there are still traces of his wish to connect the
Homeric Gods with the Old and New Testaments. The last chapters on
ethics, politics and literary and scientific subjects sum up volume three
of the *Studies*. He makes moderate claims and one misses the personal
note that appeared in the *Studies*. He still claims that the best British
and European ideas have come by way of classical Greece from Homer
– 'among the soundest of them we reckon the power of opinion and
persuasion as opposed to force; the sense of responsibility in governing
men; the hatred, not only of tyranny, but of all unlimited power; the
love and habit of public in preference to secret action'.[74]

Gladstone might well write, 'I have never known what tedium was,
have always found time full of calls & duties, life charged with every
kind of interest'.[75] In his life, religious observances, political and literary
activity jostle together with encounters with women, strange personal

crises, even recourse again to the scourge, lessons to the children or visits to the eldest at Eton or Oxford, later their political careers or marriages, visits to country houses, long walks, theatre visits, music, the sinking of pit shafts or the lapping up of precise technical information from chance fellow travellers. Occupation, light or serious, was continuous. He rejected 'vacuity or dawdling'.[76]

3

Prime Minister, a Break and Prime Minister Again

1868–1881

Disraeli's popularity declined after 1867. The electorate was not much interested in his Government's Abyssinian War nor in its negotiation of the Federation of Canada. Its Church Rate Abolition Bill and Public Schools Bill had offended Tory voters without deflecting Whig, Liberal and Radical voters from established loyalties. By teaching the Tories to pass reforms Gladstone was teaching the electorate to vote Liberal. Meanwhile, he had taken up the Irish question. It was known that he had thought the ecclesiastical part of it 'within reach' since 1857 and speeches of 1865 and December 1867 had already been targeted on Ireland.[1] In 1868 he carried three resolutions on Ireland by majorities of sixty and fifty-six, so weak now was Disraeli's support in the Commons. The first committed Parliament to disestablish the Church of England in Ireland, the second and third were consequential. Gladstone acted as if he were already at the head of the Government, carrying next the Established Church (Ireland) Bill which, had it also passed the Lords, would have suspended there and then the creation of any further vested interests in the Irish Church.

Parliament was now dissolved. During his campaign before the general election Gladstone assumed an air of solidity and governmental authority and discouraged the image of the People's William. He himself was defeated in South West Lancashire and sat in the new Parliament for Greenwich instead. The Liberals' majority was estimated at something over one hundred. Disraeli resigned immediately after the election without meeting the new Parliament.

As early as February 1868 Gladstone had anticipated having to choose his men and in July considered possible Ministerial arrangements with Lord Granville. Three days later he had decided on offering the Foreign Office to Lord Clarendon and to insist on it if the Queen, whom Clarendon had offended, were to object. On 5 December the Queen had already sanctioned a firm list of nine appointments, including that of Clarendon, and provisionally sanctioned others.[2] There was nothing surprising about the names. It was the Palmerston Government as modified by Russell and changed by death and old age, with the addition of men who had come forward in the last Parliament. Russell, George Grey and Somerset were not available, Herbert and Newcastle had died. The survivors were: Gladstone himself, de Grey now Ripon (Lord President), Kimberley (Lord Privy Seal), Clarendon (Foreign Office), Argyll (India), Granville (Colonies), Cardwell (War Office), Hartington (Postmaster General) and Goschen (Poor Law Board). The new men were Robert Lowe, the 'Adullamite' of 1866, at the Exchequer, Hugh Childers at the Admiralty, H.A. Bruce at the Home Office, Chichester Fortescue as Chief Secretary for Ireland, and Page Wood, becoming Lord Hatherley, as Lord Chancellor. John Bright, as represenative of the Radicals in the Cabinet, was appointed to the Board of Trade, and was perhaps the only risk Gladstone took. The Lord Lieutenant for Ireland, not in the Cabinet, was also a new man, the young Lord Spencer. He was third choice for the position. Lord Halifax, a survivor from Palmerston's Cabinet, had been approached but was not prepared to be in the Cabinet as viceroy, with Fortescue (and his wife, the pushing Lady Waldegrave) also insisting on the Cabinet or resenting being left out of it. Hartington had also declined. But Spencer with his wealth, status (a great landowner) and public respect was a 'natural' viceroy and had no claim yet on a Cabinet place.[3]

The Cabinet was small and harmonious. It was also well balanced: age against youth, seven between thirty-five and forty-five, eight fifty or over; Lords against Commons – six in the Lords, nine in the Commons; Oxford and Cambridge against non-university men – seven were Oxford men, two Cambridge, Bright, Bruce and Ripon the chief non-university men. Wales (Bruce), Scotland (Argyll), Ireland (Fortescue), the North (Hartington), the East (Kimberley) and the Midlands (Bright) were all represented.

Its initial success owed much to Gladstone. He showed himself a very great Prime Minister. He was great as the chairman of Cabinet, which he did not normally dominate, sacrificing much to induce that approximation of opinions which at first involved the active contribution of every member to all it was doing. He was great as the manager of legislation in the House of Commons. In 1866 and other years there had been attempts at Irish legislation, but it took Gladstone and his debating and drafting skill as well as his majority to pass bills at last. The House of Lords, with its Tory majority, would have preferred still to resist. Gladstone showed his greatness in managing conflict through his friends and allies without ever provoking last-ditch resistance. He had no wish to reform the House of Lords, telling Granville that he was an out and out inegalitarian. His enemies might call him 'the imperious Minister'[4] but that was not the inside view.

The Irish Church Establishment Bill was first discussed in the Cabinet on 8 February 1869 and its form finally settled on the 22nd. It passed its second reading in the Commons with a vote of '368:250, a notable & historic division', as Gladstone called it, and then after being eleven nights in committee it went to the Lords where it passed its second reading in June. The struggle between Lords and Commons then began. The Commons amended the Lords' amendments and returned the bill much in its first form. It finally passed (23 July) after a compromise was negotiated by Granville, primed and directed throughout by Gladstone, with the Archbishops of Canterbury and York and Lords Cairns and Salisbury for the Tory Opposition. 'A woeful huckstering affair', Gladstone called it since the crux at the end was money. The Opposition wanted at least three million to float the new Church.[5]

The matters in dispute concerned, first, the relations between State and Church. Gladstone led the Cabinet in resisting the use of the resources of the Protestant British state to endow the Roman Catholic or Presbyterian Church. What was called 'concurrent endowment' was a non-starter. That the Protestant state should not endow Catholic or nonconformist institutions was a tenet he consistently applied all his life. He drew a typically narrow distinction between 'endowment of' and 'grants of money to'. The second matter related to property. The property of the old established Church of England in Ireland had been mostly in the form of the life interests of the clergy in buildings or land, glebe land and the Ulster glebe houses and endowments from royal grants since 1560. The financial clauses, giving money for the life interests and the glebe lands and glebe houses, could be either more or less favourable to the new Irish Church, a corporate body under Commissioners. Any surplus money might be applied to the relief of poverty or economic projects. The scope, then, which these matters gave for dispute and compromise will be easily understood. In addition, the bill raised the question of the functions and composition of the

House of Lords. Russell offered the Lords in June a bill for the creation of life peerages. John Bright in a letter to his Birmingham constituents (10 June) threatened that the existence of the Lords would be endangered if it rejected the Irish Church bill.

Gladstone's commitment next involved him in the problem of Irish land on which he worked in 1869 and passed an act in 1870. English land law and Irish land law were not intrinsically different but the conditions within which each operated were entirely different. Irish agriculture did not admit of capital development but not because of 'wicked' absentee landlords. Some might be sometimes in England, some might be unable to live on all their scattered estates at once. They were isolated rather than 'wicked' and even this isolation can be exaggerated. They were, in fact, caught in the same intractable conditions as their tenants. Ireland was a land of tenant farmers. The freeholders and long- or short-term leaseholders present in England were largely absent from Ireland. Moreover, the size of their tenancies was extremely small whereas the landlords were few and the size of their estates extremely large. This not only made it impossible for tenants to bargain with landlords but the very smallness of their farms was an important bar to capital development. Farms were increasing in size, but the population was rising and this introduced the complicating factor of land-hunger with always another man ready to take the place of a tenant who could not pay his rent. In 1861 Irish farms exceeding 100 acres (the average size in England) were only 5 per cent of all holdings above one acre and only one-sixth of the remaining 95 per cent exceeded fifty acres. Farms of ten, twenty or thirty acres were most normal and farms of one acre were not unusual. If the landlord cleared his land by evictions and let it out in bigger units he would solve his economic problem, but this landlords were, in fact, reluctant to do. An even more important factor in the conditions obstructing capital development was the prevalence of a notion of property rights which left the landlord's property in his land incomplete. It was contested by the tenant's claim that he, too, had property in the land and that this should be reflected in his rent. This was not the same as the English translation that the landlord should demand only a fair and fixed rent. The tenant also believed that his property in the land gave him rights to divide and sublet (though this practice was on the decline), to pass to his heirs, to sell his right in it, to hold on a yearly basis yet in fact to stay for as long as he wished or to leave after the year. Tenant right was not the same as the English translation of it into the limited right to sell to the next man the improvements he might have made during his tenancy, nor even the translation into 'security of tenure'. In short, the whole context of Irish agriculture was dominated by custom and claims rather than written contract or agreed leases or what might be called the market mind. The Irish tenant mostly 'lived outside a system of cash payments'.[6]

Gladstone's Irish land bill was a feeble measure. It was a classic example of too much discussion and too many contributions from too many men. The discussions took the whole imaginative force out of an original plan. At Gladstone's invitation, no fewer than eight members of the Cabinet produced whole schemes at an advanced stage of discussion and after he had abandoned his own coherent and far-reaching scheme (much diminishing the landlord's property in the land), presented to the Cabinet on 30 October 1869.[7] John Bright also had a radical solution: state-aid to buy out the landlords. On 21 May 1869 he had written to Gladstone proposing precisely such a scheme with even an element of compulsion. Gladstone had rejected it out of hand (22 May). 'By Bright's plan,' wrote Granville, summing up its impossibility, 'not only would the State assume the responsibilities to the tax payer of a great land jobbing speculation, but it would place itself in the odious position of a landlord exacting more than the average rent from the whole population'.[8] A clause in the bill, allowing the tenant to purchase with a State loan provided he laid down 25 per cent of the purchase money, was all that was left of Bright's idea and it was to take three more pieces of legislation and a quarter of a century before the solution of peasant proprietorship was effective.

Discussion continued involving both the press and the Tory Chief Secretary of 1868. The limited bill which Gladstone introduced into the Commons on 15 February 1870 recognized and legalized tenant right only by legalizing the Ulster custom outside Ulster. This was a customary tenure likened to copyhold in England. It gave the tenant property in his improvements. It avoided the radical solution of giving universal protection to tenant right and legalizing whatever was customary everywhere. It provided for compensation for disturbance if rent had been paid and it incorporated the land purchase clause already referred to. It succeeded politically because it was so moderate. Nevertheless it might have revived (had it not been for the Franco-Prussian War) the dangerous question of the functions and composition of the House of Lords because after Granville moved its second reading there (14 June), and especially when it went into committee, the Tory majority proceeded to amend it. Amendments were to the disadvantage of the tenants or directed to safeguards against their misuse of what the bill gave them. Gladstone had 'to cram dishes of the Lords amendments down the throat of our men' when it came back to the Commons but was still not successful in preventing conflict. The Lords insisted on some changes which the Commons refused. Granville and Halifax worked on Richmond and Cairns in the Lords but on these questions of detail it was the Commons which, under Gladstone's astute guidance in cabinet and parliamentary debate, eventually gave way. The bill passed in August 1870.

In December 1868, at the very beginning of the new Government, Fortescue was sounded by John La Touche asking whether he should offer Harristown, Co. Kildare, as an Irish Balmoral.[9] With Gladstone's agreement, Fortescue discouraged him, but the offer was not finally declined until April 1869. The idea of a royal residence in Ireland had its attractions and came up again in various forms. It might appease the Irish and quieten English complaints about the Queen's reluctance to perform public duties. It might allow the viceroyalty to be abolished and Irish administration to be simplified. If the viceroyalty were abolished the Prince of Wales might reside in Ireland and find employment there and so no longer 'vapour away the prime of his life'.[10] Nothing came of the idea since the Queen made clear her dislike and Spencer was critical.

In the same conciliatory mood the Government began an experiment of governing Ireland without the exceptional powers possessed since 1865, which were thought by many to be justified by the explosions at Manchester and Clerkenwell (1867), engineered by the Fenians.[11] But during the autumn and winter of 1868, murders, threatening letters and house visits from armed parties had revived in Westmeath and neighbouring counties. Spencer appealed for power to suspend habeas corpus in disturbed districts, both officially and in letters to Granville and eventually to Gladstone himself. He was supported in the Cabinet by Fortescue, Hartington, Cardwell, Bruce and Argyll.[12] Gladstone had 'an invincible dislike' of coercion. [13] He hedged at every turn and once even proposed that the young Kimberley, viceroy in 1864–66, should be first sent to enquire. It was not until April 1870 that the Peace Preservation (Ireland) Act gave Spencer rather less than he asked for and not until June 1871 that the Protection of Life and Property Act, the Westmeath Act, gave him power to suspend habeas corpus. Thus the experiment ended and Gladstone's hope that Ireland could be reconciled to British rule by trust and goodwill was falsified.

Finally he introduced a bill for the reform of Irish university education, It was very much his own measure. The plan was to group the Queen's Colleges of Cork and Belfast, the Presbyterian Magee College, Londonderry, Newman's Roman Catholic College and Trinity College, Dublin, in a revived federal University of Dublin. However, the federal idea was remote both from Catholic Ireland and from the proud traditions of the well-endowed Protestant Trinity College, Dublin. The new university was to be governed by an interdenominational Council and to be financed partly by the State, partly by endowments of Trinity and partly by fees. The Catholic College was not to be endowed. The religious test at Trinity was to be abolished and the teaching of theology, moral philosophy and history banned. The bill was defeated by a combination of Tories, Irish members and Liberal dissentients of Whiggish views. Thereupon the Government resigned (13 March 1873). It was compelled to resume office on 17 March since Disraeli declined the Queen's commission.

To balance this Gladstonian failure there was a Gladstonian achievement – the abolition of the religious tests at Oxford and Cambridge. A bill for this purpose had been introduced in both 1869 and 1870 but failed. The bill of 1871 succeeded, because it was taken as a major measure, introduced by Gladstone himself on the first day of the session and carried through by his persuasive force. Much the same might be said of the ballot. The bill introducing the secret ballot at parliamentary elections and the Corrupt Practices Bill both failed in 1871. In 1872 Gladstone managed a new bill, defeating proposals for making the secret ballot optional and foiling other opposition by inserting the essential part of the Corrupt Practices Bill into the ballot bill and abandoning the rest. Provision for entry into the Civil Service for all departments except the Foreign Office may also be ascribed to Gladstone. It substituted competitive examinations for the old qualifying examinations which the Civil Service Commission he had thought of in 1854 (see p. 29) administered.

Gladstone did not begin the administration of 1868–74 with a legislative plan. He had nothing similar to the programme of 1856. He also handled his Cabinet with a loose grip, but his methods were extremely businesslike. He was the first Prime Minister to have a Cabinet agenda. It was private to himself, written in his own hand in a standard form and with decisions on some topics sometimes interlined. The Cabinet met regularly during the parliamentary session, normally on a Saturday to arrange the weekly parliamentary business and irregularly in a series of out-of-session planning meetings in November–December to arrange the next session.[14] The loose grip meant that other major legislative achievements of the Government may all legitimately be ascribed to individual Ministers. One notices that in all this legislative work, at the stage when bills came before the Cabinet, for example over the Irish University bill and in his plan which failed over Irish land, Gladstone's personal leaning was towards radical solutions. There is a list after a Cabinet note in 1873 of subjects on which 'divisions in the Liberal party may be seriously apprehended'. It ends: 'On these questions generally my sympathies are with what may be termed the advanced party, whom, on other & general grounds, I certainly will never heed or lead'.[15]

Much the most prominent of individual achievements was Forster's Education Act of 1870. By the mid-sixties there was consensus that both elementary and endowed schools were inadequate, especially in the cities, both in quantity and in character. The State grant to the voluntary schools had been increased to £840,000 by 1862 and the 'revised code' provided by the committee of the Privy Council on education had broached the problem of quality. Disraeli's Public Schools Act had opened up the question of endowments and their use by the older schools. By the end of the decade there was growing agreement that local authorities should be allowed to use ratepayers' money to finance new schools. In 1869 Argyll's Scottish Schools Bill, though it failed in the Lords, passed Cabinet and Commons without arousing bitterness, and an important Endowed Schools Bill was enacted. Forster was author of the English Schools Bill and its manager through Cabinet and Parliament. In the Commons Gladstone lent important procedural help and gave way to him when they differed. He introduced his bill on 17 February 1870, the earliest possible day. He then had to take it through at the same time as Gladstone was taking the Irish land bill through. The heavy and intricate timetable taxed both his skill and that of colleagues and the temper of the Liberal majority. In April the tussle began with the Tory majority in the Lords and continued until the beginning of August. When enacted, it allowed school boards to be elected by local initiative wherever the number of schools was shown to be inadequate. School boards were empowered to levy a rate for the establishment and maintenance of Board Schools. The Board Schools were not secular but were to provide religious teaching. The Cowper-Temple amendment, a compromise arrived at uneasily, prohibited the teaching of particular formularies or catechisms. Gladstone with others had resisted this compromise as 'an absurdity'. But the act was W.E. Forster's and not his.

Similarly, Gladstone's old Peelite colleague, Edward Cardwell, was responsible for drafting, persuading Cabinet and Commons and generally managing army reform. He had, indeed, won a place in 1871 for this measure in the legislative programme because his plans were ready.[16] He had to fit the Army Regulation Bill in with the Univeristy Tests Bill, which was having a difficult passage, together with the first version of the ballot bill. The Army Regulation Bill demanded the detailed and special knowledge of the Secretary for War and his department and Gladstone did not intervene over its substance. He himself had wished for a more radical reform compelling officers, for example, to serve in the ranks before being commissioned, but gave way to Cardwell's professional views. He noted Cardwell's 'signal and merited success' with his initial statement, deplored the effort to obstruct its passage with motions for adjournment, and spoke at length on the second reading and on its final passage.[17] He made more than one constructive suggestion on procedure and when the Lords in July rejected the provision of the bill for the abolition, with compensation, of the purchase of officers' commissions, he conducted the correspondence with the Commander-in-Chief and the Queen which arranged the alternative method of abolishing it by Royal Warrant. The Lords, understanding that under this there would be no compensation, hastened to pass the Army Regulation Bill.

The Home Secretary, H.A. Bruce, was responsible for the Trade Union legislation of 1871 and the Licensing Bill of 1872. Bruce had been stirred to action by Gladstone's promise of Government legislation made to two private members, Tom Hughes and A.J. Mundella, to persuade them to withdraw their radical bill in 1870. Bruce's timid bill, eventually divided into two, was not well managed in the Cabinet, nor vigorously debated in the Commons. The Criminal Law Amendment Act did not amend Disraeli's Masters and Servants Act and the act of picketing, when shown to be 'watching and besetting', remained a criminal offence. The Trade Union Act gave trade societies full protection for their funds by allowing them to register with the Registrar of Friendly Societies. Gladstone sympathized with Hughes's and Mundella's attempt to give the Trade Unions security for their funds and saw to it, when their first bill was abandoned in July 1869, that Bruce had parliamentary time to enact a temporary bill giving them security for a year. The much disliked provision in relation to picketing

– the Criminal Law Amendment Act – seems to have been Bruce's individual decision. Bruce mentioned to Gladstone consultation with the Attorney General, but did not go into particulars.[18] Licensing legislation had worried Bruce throughout 1871 and he had ready in April 1872 only 'a confused mass of absurdity' which he suggested Kimberley should take over and introduce first into the Lords to get it through in that session.[19] This was done and in its final form the bill, which alienated the publicans and brewing interest without attaching the temperance people, was the work of Kimberley and Thring, the parliamentary Counsel. One of the early measures of the next Government, the 'Additional Facilities for Drunkenness Bill', as Gladstone called it, again extended the opening hours which Bruce had restricted.[20]

The overhaul of the 'Superior Courts' had been among bills to be prepared from the autumn of 1869 but it was not until Selborne replaced Hatherley as Lord Chancellor in October 1872 that anything was done. Behind the Judicature Act of 1873 lay his drafting skill and force. The Act overshot the mark in abolishing the appellate jurisdiction of the House of Lords – it was restored by Cairns's Act under the next Government – but was otherwise one of the Government's most successful measures.

Among the achievements of Gladstone in this administration may be counted foreign policy, for it bore the stamp of Gladstone's mind, perhaps less so under Clarendon than under Granville who took office on Clarendon's death in July 1870. Any vigour the policy had was the product of Gladstone's idealism on one side and his legalism on the other. He did not believe that foreign policy was about power in Europe nor about the protection of British interests. He believed foreign policy should be about justice among the peoples and was prepared 'to throw overboard these special interests. I do not believe in them'.[21] He also believed that foreign policy was the application to foreign affairs of general ideas and the rule of law. It was an interpretation on which he could unite the Whigs and Radicals without satisfying either of them. But he could generally carry the House of Commons with him though not always the Cabinet. He lost some support over the Black Sea Conference in 1871 but, in comparison with his second administration, policy in 1869–74 showed both consistency of thinking and suitability to the situation.

It was again to Rome that Gladstone gave the primacy, though not in quite the same sense as in 1859. It is interesting that Gladstone had

had an audience of Pius IX in 1866, and in a long conversation had discussed both Irish and Roman affairs in general terms.[22] In Rome in 1869 preparations for the Vatican Council and the Declaration of Papal Infallibility were going on. For Gladstone the Declaration would annul a hope he had of the reunion of the Churches and 'it cast in doubt the civic allegiance of all Roman Catholic populations'.[23] He had convinced himself that Pius IX had revived the whole papal policy of the reign of Elizabeth I and was again using the very same instruments which had justified her in fighting the treasonable intentions of Roman Catholics. He published in 1874 *The Vatican Decrees in their reading of Civil Allegiance,* to expose this policy. In 1869 he wished to encourage European intervention in Rome to prevent the Declaration. Both Bavaria and France made moves at Rome in the direction Gladstone favoured, but there was never any likelihood that either would be successful with or without British participation. The Council ended when the Franco-Prussian War broke out. French troops, which had occupied Rome since 1859, were withdrawn. But the Declaration was formulated and issued as the Council was brought to an end.

Just before war was declared, Clarendon was engaged in delicate pressure upon Bismarck at the instance of the French foreign minister, to reduce the size of the Prussian army. Only the Queen and Gladstone knew about the secret disarmament negotiations of February to March 1870. It was a part of Clarendon's policy with which he entirely sympathized, even if it failed as it was bound to do. By the date war was declared (15 July) Clarendon had died and Granville replaced him. Granville had been Colonial Secretary and worked closely with Gladstone over the Red River rebellion in Canada, for example, in principle pursuing the Gladstonian policy of colonies being responsible for their own external defence and withdrawing British troops, but in actual conditions giving military assistance to Canada in crushing the rebellion. Granville was Gladstone's ally in the Cabinet and now shaped his foreign policy in close partnership with him. Foreign Office correspondence, with Gladstone's emendations to drafts, and their private correspondence show how often Gladstone provided the ideas and Granville the negotiating skills and conciliatory temper which carried them out.

On the outbreak of the Franco-Prussian War Britain at once proclaimed her neutrality. Both Bismarck and Napoleon III tried to win British public opinion. To this end, Bismarck communicated to Gladstone (19 July) through the Prussian ambassador in London, the so-called Benedetti Treaty, asking a promise of secrecy. This was the draft of a treaty which the French ambassador in 1866 had been ambitious and vain enough to hope he might induce Bismarck to sign. It would have given France territorial compensation at the expense of Belgium for Prussian aggrandizement. Gladstone, contrary to Bismarck's expectation, kept the secret and a week later (25 July) Bismarck published the treaty in *The Times*. The whole incident was insignificant unless it made it easier to get a vote of credit from Parliament or strengthened Gladstone in 'forming Engagements about Belgium'.[24] British neutrality was made safer by the treaties signed on 9 August with Prussia and 11 August with France by which each undertook to respect Belgian neutrality. Granville had thought it might be 'wise' to ask Prussia and France if they were prepared to respect the neutrality of Belgium but had had second thoughts and done nothing. It was only when Gladstone took up the idea that it solidified into treaties of three articles, of which he had proposed the substance and amended the drafts, taking care that they should not weaken the 1839 treaty.[25] The treaties were rightly associated with him rather than Granville and not merely because it was he who defended them in the House of Commons.

When after Sedan and the fall of Napoleon III at the beginning of September the Provisional Government of the French Third Republic began to sue for peace, Gladstone protested against its policy of 'not an inch of our territory, and not a stone of our fortresses' to be surrendered. While Granville put Bismarck and Jules Favre in touch at Ferrières and listened to Thiers when he toured the European capitals begging for help, in fact he did nothing, refusing to mediate or to commit Britain to any opinion. Gladstone, on the other hand, wished to protest against the Prussian demand for Alsace-Lorraine. He pressed for this protest more vigorously than he had pressed for a protest against French intransigence and he did not think that the two protests went in opposite directions. There was a distinction between the annexation of the people of a whole province without their consent and claiming fortresses or frontier adjustment as the legitimate price of victory. It was a characteristically narrow Gladstonian distinction, but one notices again, as over Belgium, the general idea which he wished to apply, successfully or not, of national self-determination. Gladstone appealed to the Cabinet against Granville. But the specially summoned meeting of 30 September rejected his proposal and so did those of 12 October and 23 November when he renewed it.[26] His article 'Germany, France

and England' in the *Edinburgh Review* for October 1870 was the vehicle
for deprecating the French intransigence and deploring the declared
intention of Germany to annex Alsace-Lorraine.

Gladstone's intuition in 1856 that the neutralization of the Black Sea
as part of the 'line of circumvallation' which Palmerston wished to build
round Russia would not stand (see p. 32) was proved correct when on
9 November 1870 Russia repudiated the Black Sea Clauses of the Treaty
of Paris. Britain had no real choice between acquiescence and calling
to life the tripartite guarantee of Turkey by Austria, France and itself,
which would have meant war against Russia – impossible to declare
when France was being invaded and occupied by Germany. Gladstone,
however, found not perhaps a third way, but at least a way of exacting
some price for acquiescence. Gladstone drafted the text of the British
reply to the Russian communication of 9 November. He evaded its
substance but argued with its words. These justified the Russian
repudiation by infractions of the Treaty of Paris which had already
taken place.[27] Gladstone asserted that treaties were valid, even if
broken, unless and until they were revised by international agreement.
This was the line of policy which procured: (1) the Protocol condemning
the unilateral denunciation of treaties of January 1871; (2) the six
sittings of the Conference of London which ended in March with the
revision of the Treaty of Paris, not only in the Russian sense, but also
giving compensation to Turkey by renewing the closure of the Straits
and recognizing its sovereign rights in the Black Sea equally with those
of Russia; and (3) the renewal by the Conference of the 1856 European
commission to supervise the navigation of the Danube for another
twelve years. The presence of France at the fifth, penultimate sitting of
the Conference was, of course, a European recognition of the Third
Republic's membership of the European Concert. One notices again
Gladstone's preoccupation with general principle, as if foreign policy
were about international right and justice rather than about power.

The fall of Napoleon III brought into question the future of the 1860
Cobden Treaty. Cobden had particularly associated the Emperor with
the treaty by making his first approaches to him and helping him to
overcome the resistance of French protectionists. The Third Republic
began with a protectionist revival and anyhow needed revenue both to
meet the costs of the war and the indemnity which Germany exacted in
the Treaty of Frankfurt of May 1871. France did not levy an income tax
and had to look to export and import duties to provide the extra
revenue. It accordingly announced a revised tariff. The ten-year period

for which the Cobden Treaty had been signed would expire in 1870, but since neither party had given the required year's notice of non-continuation it might be automatically renewed. The first question argued, then, between Britain and France was whether France's proposed new duties were protective and therefore required the revision or the discontinuance of the treaty, or were for revenue purposes only and therefore compatible with its continuance. This argument did not break down until July 1872. The new duties, suspended until then, were enforced and France gave notice of the termination of the treaty. Gladstone refused to bargain tariff for tariff, arguing that Britain's remaining wine and spirit duties were for revenue and social purposes only. Yet − and once again by a narrow Gladstonian distinction − he found the formula which allowed the re-negotiation of the Cobden Treaty. Britain wished to relieve France in her financial difficulty, she objected to protective duties but 'does not close the door to them'.[28] On that basis a new treaty allowing for the increase of the French duties while leaving the British duties as they were in 1860, and assuring her most-favoured-nation treatment, was signed on 5 November 1872. The French Chamber refused to ratify the treaty and Britain had to be content with a French Declaration of 22 January 1873. The Cobden Treaty did not in fact expire until 1882. One notices how Gladstone had preserved his free-trade idealism while applying his doctrines of approximation and adaptation to acquiesce in what was in effect a revival of French protectionism.

When Gladstone became Prime Minister Britain had a long-standing dispute with the United States arising from its having allowed the *Alabama* and other ships to use British ports to supply the South with arms during the Civil War. All attempts to settle it, including Clarendon's proposals of arbitration, had so far failed and no advantage could possibly be derived from the dispute's being allowed to drag on. But the North had won the Civil War and Britain, in so far as it had inclined to the South, must, therefore, be in the wrong. It will be recalled that no one had been more publicly in favour of the South than Gladstone at Newcastle in 1862 (see p. 38). Gladstone's immense letter to the American Minister in London about J.L. Motley, who had been provoked publicly to call him a 'liar' over this, is one of the most characteristic of Gladstonian curiosities.[29] If the dispute were submitted to arbitration no one by 1870–72 expected the award to be favourable or the indemnity, if it was unfavourable, to be small. Granville's achievement lay in getting the negotiation going again, in bringing it to an end without being provoked by American invective and at the same time bringing the dispute of Canada with the United States about fisheries and the San Juan boundary to a settlement. The important achievement was the Treaty of Washington of 8 May 1871 which governed the conditions and scope of the arbitration at Geneva on the *Alabama* and other claims. But the negotiations for this treaty had only moved forward when Gladstone supplied the distinction which allowed Britain to agree to a near-apology being inserted in its preamble. He pointed out that there was a difference between a claim for damages that one might legitimately refuse and an expression of regret that an incident had happened that one could not reasonably deny. It was a distinction that Granville could only understand when he had translated it into the homely analogy of pigeons taking the cattle plague from his farm to another man's for which he might refuse compensation, but yet regret that they had done so.[30] The fighting point in the negotiation was article VI, worded as if to govern all future behaviour of neutrals towards a country with civil war but used retrospectively by the arbitrators to give their award against Britain. To Gladstone this fixing of international behaviour for the future was adequate compensation for the four rules of article VI being turned against Britain. After the treaty was signed, the topic of argument became the so-called indirect claims. The United States claimed that by allowing the ships to sail from its ports Britain was responsible for the prolongation of the war and all the costs that arose from that. The argument produced a most acrimonious exchange of note after note during 1872. Under cover of this intransigence an informal exchange of ideas was kept going by Granville's good humour and Gladstone's inventiveness. The timetable laid down by the Treaty of Washington could thus be kept. The Tribunal of Arbitration was appointed, arbitrators named, cases presented in January and counter-cases in April. Gladstone's contribution was to keep the informal argument to the wording of the Treaty of Washington and to suppress the substantive matter of the indirect claims. These claims were, in the end, kept outside the scope of the arbitration by agreement between the Counsels on each side and by a supplementary article to the Treaty of Washington. The arbitrators gave their verdict in August and Britain became liable for an indemnity of £3 million. The establishment of good Anglo-American relations was more important than the arbitration itself, and to this Gladstone certainly contributed.

The failures in this Government were financial, legislative and, in the last analysis, political. Robert Lowe, Chancellor of the Exchequer, had utilitarian ideas, faith in the power of intellect and a distrust of popular judgement; but he did not achieve financial success. His relations with Gladstone were not easy. His first cautious and circumspect budgets were good, that of 1869, in which he achieved a 'list of things still to be done' which Gladstone sent him, particularly so. But by 1871 both the need for more revenue and a sense that time was running out led Lowe to bring forward more radical ideas. He was dissuaded by Gladstone from making his currency plan part of the budget or even introducing it as a separate bill. He proposed new taxes on gas and on matches, some alteration of the death duties and one penny on the income tax. The last Gladstone accepted, criticized the death duty changes, doubted whether the Commons would accept a tax on gas, but 'the lucifer matches I hope & think you would carry'.[31] In the event, protest that the match tax would cut down jobs in the manufacture of matches meant that Lowe was defeated and the budget had to be withdrawn – a step without precedent for an established government with a good majority. Lowe was unable to induce the defence ministers to cut their estimates and was compelled instead to put 2d on the income tax. He had two more budgets in 1872 and 1873 but was moved to the Home Office in August 1873 after the irregularities over the Zanzibar contract and the use of Post Office Savings Bank money were put down to weak supervision of the Treasury. Remarkably, Gladstone himself now became Chancellor of the Exchequer.

The legislative failure was as nothing, of course, when set beside the Ministry's achievement. It existed only in relation to the legislative zeal among both ministers and private members. Even had Gladstone come to office with an overall plan for the legislative work of the Government this zeal would have caused difficulty; without such a plan it was difficult to satisfy. The great failures were failures to cope with rating ('local taxation'), the English land laws and Scottish grievances. When, owing to the pressure on parliamentary time, bills had to be abandoned, the first to go were always those for Scotland. There were, in addition, at least two great consolidating bills (on mines and merchant shipping) which the Board of Trade had prepared and failed to gain time for. Rating and local government seemed tractable. In 1867, when the reform bill was going through, all the discussion about rating had drawn public attention to the anomalies of the system. Goschen had come to the Poor Law Board as 'a new man', the son of a banker, noted for his ability. He opened the 1869 session with a bill to provide a common basis throughout England and Wales for the valuation of property liable to rates, a similar bill for London and a bill for a minor amendment to the law for those occupying property for a term shorter than a quarter. He also introduced soon afterwards a bill to set up financial boards in the counties – foreshadowing the later County Councils. Only the bill for London was enacted. Goschen had underestimated the difficulties of his subject and the committee stage showed it. The other bills were withdrawn before the end of the session and Gladstone wrote that it was too soon to approach county government. A similar attempt to deal with valuation in Scotland failed on 1870. Again, a bill to make the incidence of the poor rate fairer in London was all that passed. Goschen had drawn on himself the antagonism of the landowning interest in the Cabinet was well as Parliament, for he wished the landlords to pay more and the occupiers less. In 1871 the Poor Law Board became the Local Government Board with a reforming and active Under-Secretary, James Stansfeld, (appointed its president in 1873) and Goschen tried and failed again. Goschen worked on his plan for elective County Councils (Boards) and the reform of London's government but could get nothing done. Gladstone promised to review the whole question of local taxation and local government during the summer recess of 1872. In 1873 a better-digested scheme for a uniform basis of valuation, standardized liability and a consolidated rate was brought in by Stansfeld and Goschen. It was thrown out on its second reading by the Lords 'with little ceremony'.[32] It is not surprising then, that the rates figured in the plan which was to lie behind the 'snap dissolution' of 1874.

The reform of the land law in England and Wales was a lawyers' subect. Politically, it was dangerous because, like rating, it divided the Whig from the Radical wing of the party by opening up the division of interest between country landowner and owner of city premises. With education and further parliamentary reform it was included in the 1873 list of subjects likely to divide the party. As the lawyers saw it, the law needed tidying up in three branches: conveyancing or transfer, inheritance and settlements. A bill on succession to land was introduced in 1870 but abandoned. In 1871 the Cabinet intended to deal with conveyancing but any attempt was crowded out by the pressure of other business. In 1872, land transfer, inheritance and settlement appeared on Gladstone's lists both of subjects crowded out and of things to be attempted in 1873. By then, Selborne had brought fresh energy and reforming zeal to the chancellorship. In the planning cabinets of November it was decided that he should prepare a bill on land transfer and introduce it early in the session into the House of Lords. This was confirmed in January. By April Selborne had brought a Land Title and Transfer Bill and a Real Property Limitation Bill to the Cabinet and no objection was made to his introducing them into the Lords as they stood. No more was heard of these bills and the Judicature Act (see p. 61) was the sum of Selborne's achievement.

The greatest failure was political. About 1868 the machinery of government and the Civil Service especially was just entering upon one of its phases of phenomenal expansion and departments were developing independence and self-consciousness. It would perhaps have been impossible to continue under the new weight of business the old informality of cabinet and government method much longer. Add to this that the Reform Act of 1867 had brought into the Commons a type of private member, there not in an old-fashioned way to play the party game nor even to support Gladstone or Disraeli but in a new-fashioned way to cut a figure and to advance a legislative cause of his own, under contract to his constituency (a word now used in its modern sense) to devote his time and energies to public business. The temper of the House had changed. Attendance was higher than it had ever been, but attendance at government divisions, or sitting through the night to vote for a government measure was more difficult to obtain from members of the Government, let alone from back-benchers. Before 1871 Gladstone had lost his hold upon the Liberal back-benchers. By one great speech he could recapture them, but for ordinary plodding business they were not to be won over.

Legislative congestion was the trouble. The large number of government bills, the arrears when a proportion of these failed and had to be reintroduced, the large number of private members' bills, the increase in bills coming under general acts as provisional orders or schemes, all these things threw the parliamentary timetable into chaos. This in turn produced more discouragement and more abandonment of bills, more late-night sittings, count-outs and ultimately government defeats. Gladstone's proposals to relieve congestion by establishing permanent committees to take certain kinds of bills came to nothing. Some relief was achieved by taking more bills through the Lords first. The fine majority on which Gladstone could rely in 1869 had halved, and in 1871 and often afterwards he was working with a majority of some fifty only. In 1871 the Liberals began to lose by-elections on a serious scale. Gladstone had alienated whole sections of his supporters outside the House. There was some improvement inside the House in 1872 and pressure on parliamentary time was a little relaxed, but 1873 was even worse than 1871 and culminated in the defeat of the Government on the Irish University Bill. There followed Disraeli's refusal to form a government and Gladstone's return with a dead session in front of him and only Cardwell's and Kimberley's expedition to the Gold Coast (over which he was ignored) to hold public interest.

He brought the administration to an end with the apparently snap decision to dissolve, thought of on 18 January and swiftly applied on 23 January 1874. It was not quite what it appeared to be. It was Gladstone's bold and astute answer to Disraeli's clever holding back from office in 1873. He intended to go to the electorate with 'a daring and dramatic plan' to use a budget surplus of £5 million to make a radical change in the taxation system. The plan was to do three things at once: (1) to relieve the ratepayer by relieving the localities of expenses in proportion as they paid house tax and licensing fees; (2) to relieve the income taxpayer by abolishing income tax and making up the revenue with legacy and succession duties; and (3) to ensure economies from the spending departments. His main argument against the income tax was that it encouraged expenditure because it brought revenue in too easily. To abolish it would put a straitjacket on the spending departments. The plan had been slowly developed since the autumn. When dissolution was proposed to the Cabinet it was 'thought of as an escape from a difficulty' just arisen with the service Ministers over their high estimates. But within days Gladstone saw that the taxation plan made 'it the best thing in itself'.[33] Income tax abolition plus some £800,000 off the rates was Gladstone's offer to the electorate. His plan deserved to succeed. But the electorate was not interested. It could afford to pay and saving money had no appeal. The elections were over on 12 February. The Tories had carried some 352 seats to the Liberals' 243, with the fifty-seven more or less independent Irish members being reckoned with the Liberals.

Gladstone's first Government seemed to have failed. Its power had certainly declined after 1871. But its achievement in the mark it left on Ireland, on the schools, on the army, on the law courts (even by new buildings in the Strand), on the Church, on the universities, on the Civil Service, on the trade union movement, on almost all British institutions, was outstanding. There had also been a great deal of legislative activity among private members, some of it self-defeating and much of it a failure, but all of it opening up questions and often pointing the way to modernization. Administrative reform had gone on within departments and parliamentary procedure had begun to be scrutinized. Externally,

British relations with the continent and the United States were all better in 1874 than they had been in 1867. It was perhaps too much activity in too many directions that caused it to lose the election, rather than failure.

Nor must it be supposed that Gladstone's personal life was entirely absorbed in his public activity at this period. Its variety of occupations still continued. 'Relaxation and refreshment are properly to be found in the alternation of different employments' he had written in 1858 and he still acted on that principle. His intimacy with Laura Thistlethwayte came to its crisis in 1869. Gladstone's self-control had ultimately proved complete. The incident illustrated the ambiguity of a mind that 'could "court evil" while doing good'.[34]

Gladstone resigned without meeting Parliament on 17 February and tried at once to withdraw from the leadership of the Liberal Party. He was persuaded to stay on until 1875. The election programme had been his personal idea. The defeat was a personal defeat and there was an element of bruised pride in his withdrawal. Yet to the religious base of Gladstone's nature the political struggle had always been uncongenial. It is tempting to quote the almost yearly passages in his diary in which he asserts his weariness. He would do so to the end and it is difficult to know how literally to take him. Nevertheless, in 1874 his line was that the party would recover and he would retire. Though formally he did not abdicate until 1875 his virtual abdication may be dated from March 1874 for two reasons. Firstly he was an infrequent attender after dinner in the House during the whole of the 1874 session and was encouraged by Granville to stay away. The Liberals more often spoke against each other than against the Tory Government and Gladstone's presence was immediately seized upon by 'some of our disaffected' to separate themselves from him 'or any other leader'.[35] When he did speak, on the Public Worship Bill, it at once provoked Harcourt to a gratuitous display of his own theological learning, and when Gladstone administered a rebuke for this want of taste, Harcourt next day treated the House to a return match 'speaking for an hour', as Gladstone wrote, 'at me'. Secondly, Gladstone only remained leader under a kind of suspended sentence on his followers. He had circulated a letter to those accepting the Liberal Whip and wrote formally to Granville after discussion with him, saying that he 'could not contemplate any unlimited extension of active political service' and proposed 'shortly before the commencement of the Session of 1875' to consider whether he should claim release. This kind of half-and-half position was impossible because when Gladstone appeared on the front opposition bench 'no on else has any authority'.[36]

When the time came Gladstone effected his resignation by a letter to Granville dated 13 January 1875 and at once published it in the newspapers. Two things are remarkable in these transactions and those which immediately followed. The abdication was arranged through Granville, and Gladstone persistently used phrases which meant that it was abdication in Granville's favour. He handed over 'his trust' to Granville, a man unlikely ever to be his successor. A meeting of the party took place with John Bright in the chair which elected Hartington leader of the Liberal Party in the Commons. Only members of the Commons were called to this meeting and it merely ratified a decision already taken. That decision only related to the Commons. For Gladstone and Granville, Hartington sat from the beginning 'on the pillion'. Whether Hartington understood that is not clear. But he was detached, objective, public-spirited and at forty-two still young enough to wait. He was to lead the breakaway movement in 1886. It is doubtful, in any case, whether Granville, who had first been Foreign Secretary and Cabinet Minister in 1852, would have served under Hartington as Prime Minister. When in 1846 Aberdeen told Gladstone of Peel's intention to break with the Conservatives, but to stay in the Commons 'taking part in public questions as his view of public interests might from time to time seem to require', Gladstone had replied 'this for *him* & in the House of Commons was an intention absolutely impossible to fulfil. That with his greatness he could not remain there overshadowing & eclipsing all Governments & yet have to do with no government.'[37] Gladstone might with profit have applied this judgement to himself in 1875. But Gladstone like Peel — and like Achilles who withdrew from the battle but not the battlefield at Troy — kept his seat in the House of Commons.

The year 1874, then, saw the second break in Gladstone's life. The turning point of 1874 was less sharp than that of 1845. The fresh start came sooner. It was marked by the pamphlet on Turkish atrocities in Bulgaria of September 1876. The new course adopted in 1876 was a course of popular politics. Gladstone's career had still its parliamentary centre, of course, though the duel there with Disraeli was never resumed. He had gone to the Lords as Earl of Beaconsfield in 1876.

Gladstone's interest in the events which began with the revolt of the Serbs in Bosnia and Hercegovina against Turkey seems to have become acute only after Disraeli and Derby (son of the Prime Minister of 1852,

1858 and 1866–67), abandoned the policy of co-operating with the European Powers to persuade Turkey to reform her relations with her subject peoples. They sent the fleet to Besika Bay, Serbia and Montenegro declared war on Turkey and the Bulgarians joined the revolt. Gladstone talked at length on three occasions with Stratford de Redcliffe, one-time ambassador to Turkey and the greatest authority in England on the diplomacy of the Eastern Question, and he mastered the Blue Books as the Government issued them. As is usual in his diary, he makes no comment on newspaper news – except once when shocked by Disraeli's purchase of Suez Canal shares. The Liberals, stirred by the conflicting reports of atrocities against Bulgarians, forced a debate on the Government in which Gladstone 'spoke over two hours on this wide and difficult subject'.[38] He attacked the policy of isolated action pursued by the Government yet carefully avoided driving the attack home. He spoke as one who shared responsibility for the Crimean War and believed still in the old anti-Russian policy. He was, as he wrote to Granville, anxious lest the presence of an inactive fleet in Besika Bay should seem to condone the atrocities.[39] When Baring, on enquiry, confirmed the atrocious slaughter of Bulgarians, Gladstone wrote to Granville 'I hope you will make sure that the results of the enquiry will be published at once not bottled up till February' when Parliament would meet again. The session ended on 15 August: Gladstone, who had characteristically acted on the correct assumption that Parliament was the arena for the nation to challenge the Government and that it was for Granville and Hartington to lead it in doing so, was free.

A fortnight later he began to write the anti-Turk pamphlet, *Bulgarian Horrors and the Question of the East.* He wrote to Granville 'I am in half, perhaps a little more than half, a mind to write a pamphlet': mainly on the ground that Parliamentary action was all but outsted. The pamphlet, written in the heat of the moment, was ready by the 3rd and published on 6 September. John Murray put out a first edition of 20,000 but within a month 200,000 had been sold.[40] Hartington had thought the pamphlet 'unnecessary' and realized that Gladstone was wrong in saying that Parliament had been 'ousted', but both he and Granville were with him when the thing went to press. Gladstone moved with an existing public excitement and it may be true that he was more stirred by popular passion than himself stirring it. Nevertheless, the Bulgarian agitation as a historical event could not have become so important had he not concentrated it to one purpose. The thousands that signed petitions to the Queen or Foreign Office, attended meetings and voted for resolutions had now, if not a form of words, at least a single idea – the idea of Bulgarian self-government. There is, however, no denying that Gladstone had a base on which to build in existing agitation. James Lewis Farley – Gladstone had read his book on Turkish finance – had founded the League in aid of the Christians of Turkey; E.A. Freeman, the historian, after a journey to the east, began to collect money on their behalf; Canon Liddon at St Paul's and Bishop Fraser in Manchester had preached (Anglo-Catholics and Nonconformists were to be the backbone of the agitation in an unepxected alliance with rural labourers and urban trade unionists); Harcourt, Forster and Evelyn Ashley had started a committee in the Commons to watch the Eastern Question; a public meeting had already taken place in Willis's rooms on 27 July; forty-seven much larger meetings of various kinds had taken place up and down the country by 22 September; W.T. Stead of the *Northern Echo* had whipped up public opinion in the north east.[41] It is also worth noting that in the context of Gladstone's reading and writing life, resumed in 1874, a pamphlet found a natural place. The speech at Blackheath on 9 September was only a consequence of the pamphlet and he refused invitations to speak outside his Greenwich constituency though he wrote a second pamphlet. October and November were quieter but the climax of it all occurred on 8 December in the Conference on the Eastern Question at which anyone at all of note in the agitation figured as a convener.

The agitation did not change the policy of the Government. Events in the East moved on to another attempt to persuade Turkey to change her governing methods at the Conference of Constantinople and, when that failed, to the Russian declaration of war upon Turkey. Public attention inevitably changed its focus and, temporarily, the agitation died down. Nevertheless in Gladstone's life it had great importance for it marked the renewal of his relationship with the common man. He was back in the popular enthusiasm of 1861–62. Small crowds and extempore speeches became customary whenever he could be caught on the northern tour he made immediately after publishing the pamphlet, after the Blackheath speech and, again, in January 1877 during a tour of Wiltshire and Somerset. Delegations to Hawarden – 5,000 from Bolton – began again in the summer of 1877.

By 1877 Gladstone had assumed once more a prominent position in the House of Commons. But now there was no Disraeli to rebuke, answer or generally 'pitch into'. Between 8 February and 4 May 1877 Gladstone attended after dinner nine times, speaking on each occasion.

He afterwards wrote that he had 'never made so great a sacrifice to party' in giving up, at Granville's behest, a motion on Bulgaria that he wished to bring in. By April he was deep in negotiations about resolutions on the Eastern Question which he proposed to put to the House. When eventually put, on 7 May, they had been much attenuated and he had 'such a sense of solitary struggle' as he never remembered. But the old magic worked. 'House gradually came round & at the last was more than good.' Thenceforward he took an increasing number of parliamentary initiatives on an ever-widening range of subjects, attended more and more leaders' conclaves and on Indian finance was even invited by Hartington to make the intended motion.[42] From the end of the session his return to power was likely. Midlothian was to make it irresistible.

Gladstone's decision in 1878 not to stand again for Greenwich was another sign of his fresh beginning. Many constituencies would have welcomed him. He decided to stand for Midlothian County.

Of course, Gladstone as a Scotsman had an obvious reason for choosing a Scottish constituency, but as so often with Gladstone what seemed an innocent personal preference turned out to be also a most astute political move, given the failure of so many Scottish measures in his first Ministry. He was, moreover, assured both by the Whip, W.P. Adam, and Lord Moncrieff, more soberly, that he was certain of winning the seat. Others were also involved. It was at Lord Rosebery's instance that the Liberal Association in Midlothian invited him to stand. This was not Gladstone's first political dealing with the greatest Liberal landowner in the constituency. He had offered him a lordship-in-waiting in 1872 to be combined with the representation of a department in the Lords and, in 1873, he and Granville by great persuasion induced him to accept a Lord Lieutenancy. Rosebery had responded to the magic of Gladstone's intervention in the Bulgarian atrocities agitation and spoken in Gladstone's support in the House of Lords. He argued now that to win Leeds or any other city constituency would not be a striking victory, but that to win a country district regularly returning a Tory and under the political control of the Tory Duke of Buccleuch would be just the striking victory that was wanted.[43] Gladstone consulted Granville, who approved. No details of this consultation survive but the letter from Granville beginning 'You have done', by accepting the invitation, 'a very plucky & public-spirited thing' reads as if there had been even now some hesitation on Gladstone's part.[44] Once acceptance was decided upon, Gladstone concocted, with Adam's help and Granville's approval,

a reply that was also his election address. There proved in the end to
to be others besides Granville, Rosebery and Adam who had an interest
in the return of Gladstone to the lead. Both Lord Wolverton, former
Liberal Whip, and the Radicals, including Joseph Chamberlain, might
be counted as fighting with him in Midlothian. Again Gladstone came
in with the tide. Already on 2 November 1879 he believed 'the Tory
party is travelling towards a great smash'. During 1879 the Government's Afghan war provoked a minor agitation and its African
assertiveness added more fuel to the fire.

The first Midlothian campaign began on 24 November 1879 with the
characteristic crowds and extempore speeches at Carlisle and Hawick
on the way to Edinburgh. In all three of the great Midlothian orations
Gladstone did not and could not speak as anything but the greatest
Liberal figure of the day. Yet he spoke with authority, alluding to the
hope, for example, that 'the verdict of the country will give to Lord
Granville and Lord Hartington the responsible charge of affairs' (which
must have sounded as odd then as it reads now). He spoke, moreover,
not as a candidate to his constituents but as a former Prime Minister
from his constituency, to Scotland primarily, but beyond that to the
whole electorate of all the British Isles. 'Gentlemen', he said, 'from
Midlothian at present we are speaking to England as well as to
Scotland'. The campaign ended on 8 December after a number of lesser
speeches in a series of towns. A modern reader is struck not perhaps
by the magic that held thousands spellbound or reduced them to a
cheering mass, but by the power to develop a most varied set of themes
(though financial extravagance dominated) all in the same essential
direction.[45] The second campaign followed in March 1880.

The importance of this fresh start cannot be felt unless one
understands that, in order to make it, Gladstone was leaving behind the
rich literary sub-plot of his life. On retirement in 1875 he recorded an
attempt 'to lay out before' his wife 'my views about the future &
remaining section of my life . . . The main point is this: that . . . my
prospective work is not Parliamentary . . . But there is much to be done
with the pen, all bearing much on high & sacred ends, for even Homeric
study as I view of it [*sic*] is in this very sense of high importance: and
what lies beyond this is concerned directly with the great subject of
belief'.[46] Gladstone's *Homeric Synchronism: an enquiry into the Time
and Place of Homer* which came out early in 1876 was the most
important of his Homeric writings in that it led the way towards the
acceptance in Britain of the results of H. Schliemann's excavations on

the site of Troy and later at Mycene. Gladstone had met Schliemann when he came to London in the summer of 1875, heard him lecture on the excavations to the Society of Antiquaries[47] and subsequently corresponded with him. He read the English translation of Schliemann's book and German commentaries on it. In his own book he describes the findings of Schliemann's excavation at Hissarlik and gives reasons for accepting his conclusion that it was the site of Troy. It all chimes with his own earlier view of Homer's importance in enlightening the reader about the society, customs and institutions of a period just before the time at which Homer himself lived.

Homeric Synchronism has, however, importance in a second way. The discovery of papyri in Egypt of Greek authors, including Homer, belongs to some twenty years before 1875. Next came the deciphering of inscriptions in Egypt and from that the construction of a reliable chronology of the several dynasties of ancient Egypt back to some four thousand years BC. Gladstone is concerned with the nineteenth dynasty, or more precisely the years 1316 to 1226 BC; for he finds 'correspondences' between points in the Egyptian chronology and the material provided by Homer which fix these dates as respectively the earliest and latest at which the siege of Troy could have happened. He may go beyond the evidence but he vividly reflects the excitement of his contemporaries at the new world which Egyptology as well as Assyriology was opening up.

In retirement, Gladstone also resumed his literary reviewing, publishing in the *Quarterly* for October 1874 an essay on Charlotte Yonge's *Life of Bishop Patteson*. He had been much moved by this life of a South Sea missionary, murdered by the gentle people he had taught and served, as he always was moved by the lives of men and women living under strain. In 1878 he describes himself as being moved to tears when he re-read the Patteson essay before republishing it in *Gleanings of Past years*.[48] Biographical material continues to predominate in his occasional writing. He also resumed his reviewing of novels. But it is in his writing on poetry that the reader becomes most vividly aware of the excited imagination which impelled him to write and the systematizing, generalizing intellect which controlled the outcome. After Dante and Leopardi, Gladstone placed Tennyson. He had yielded early to the enchantment of his poetry and he records his excitement: 'Read Tennyson, Tennyson, Tennyson'.[49] Gladstone, of course, knew the poet since both were friends of Arthur Hallam. After Hallam's death Tennyson called on Gladstone in London. They met again in Oxford for a long talk in 1855; they both dined now and then at 'The Club', and in 1871 Gladstone made his first visit to Farringford. In 1876 Tennyson stayed at Hawarden. In the eighties there were several meetings and in 1883 they were two weeks together on a sea voyage. They talked much on Homer, Dante, Chaucer and Shakespeare. The article to which the excitement of August 1859 led was mainly concerned with the *Idylls of the King,* just published. He wrote once more on Tennyson, in 1887, when he compared the *Locksley Hall after Sixty Years* with the Locksley Hall of 1842. Gladstone was also a lover of Sir Walter Scott's poetry and novels and re-read them at times of stress as he re-read Shakespeare then, and sometimes Jane Austen.

Gladstone's historical writing may be illustrated from his reviews of the successive volumes of Theodore Martin's *Life of the Prince Consort,* written in 1875, 1876 and 1877 and amounting to a history of his own times down to 1861; or his review of Greville's *Memoirs* or his account of the political crisis of 1859–60, both contributed to the *English Historical Review* and appearing in its first two numbers. But these are all too reliant on Gladstone's own experiences to enable the reader to judge truly of his historical skills. That he can best do from Gladstone's review (1876) of G.O. Trevelyan's *Life and Letters of Lord Macaulay.* Gladstone uses this essay to criticize Macaulay's *History of England* and he does it in a way which has hardly been bettered.[50] He notices what was not widely observed until 'the Whig theory of history' became a common criticism in the twentieth century, namely that Macaulay 'judges men and institutions and events of other times by the instruments and measures' of his own time. He finds Macaulay wrong in his strictures on the Restoration clergy and he answers Macaulay sentence by sentence from an array of first-hand authorities.

The political writings may be illustrated from 'Germany, France and England' (1870) or 'Electoral Facts' (1878) or 'Russian Policy and Deeds in Turkestan' (1876). These articles are not polemical but analytical. They are not instruments in the political battle. They suggest the universal curiosity of the writer and exactitude of his information as well as giving vent to characteristic opinions. For example, in 'Germany, France and England' he considered the end of the temporal power of 'the Popedom' as 'the greatest and most fruitful' consequence of the Franco-Prussian War; 'there was something almost of miracle or of magic in the administrative perfection' of Prussia; he approves the national unification of Germany; he deplores a foreign policy in which 'might is based only upon power' as 'a degrading form of human things';

and calls upon Britain to use her greatness 'to found a moral empire upon the confidence of the nations.'[51]

His later religious writings were not published in book form or, like that on 'future retribution' from which he was called away to write on Bulgaria, never finished. The editor of the diaries only prints occasional manuscripts of theological reflection. A possible illustration of religious writing is his review of *Ecce Homo*. J.R. Seeley's work published anonymously in 1866 has its place in that questioning of the credentials of the New Testament by means of an historical approach, which characterized the late nineteenth century. Gladstone however defends Seeley's approach. The then anonymous author had rightly bidden his readers forget nearly nineteen centuries of history and imagine Christ as he might have met Him before he understood that He was also God, Ecce Homo! Behold the man![52] Two-thirds of the review showed from the Gospels the 'gradualness' of the revelation.

It is only by bearing this scholarly and literary life in mind that anyone can undertsand the extent to which the Midlothian campaigns were a fresh start for Gladstone. The Liberal Party as a whole went into the general election of April 1880 without a single unifying programme. This allowed many electors in voting Liberal to think they were voting for a second Gladstone Government, even though Granville and Hartington were still the party leaders. The size of the Liberal majority was unexpected: it was estimated at 137, but sixty-five Home Rulers had won Irish seats. The Liberal victory being unexpected on that scale had saved Gladstone from anticipating the question of whether he would take office under Granville or Hartington. The Queen, in fact, sent for Hartington, though Gladstone believed she was 'wrong' in not sending for Granville. Meanwhile Wolverton, the former Chief Whip, had been busy at Hawarden and a great demonstration in favour of Gladstone's premiership was being planned in London. But it was through Wolverton that Gladstone virtually engineerd an invitation to himself from Granville and Hartington to accept the Queen's commission. This she offered on their advice.[53] The second Gladstone Government was a far less powerful Ministry than the first. It was also less harmonious.

Gladstone seems to have formed his Government in April 1880 under the shadow of the financial scheme of 1874. It is true that the £5 million surplus revenue no longer existed. The Tories had turned Gladstone's boast of a surplus into a charge that the Liberals took more in taxes than it cost to run the country. But the essential element in the scheme, the reduction of taxation, was carried out when the 1880 budget proposed the long-awaited abolition – it had been under attack since the fifties – of the malt duty. It was converted into a beer duty, duties on light foreign wines were reduced and a penny added to the income tax. The shadow of 1874 is especially felt in the fact that Gladstone himself took the office of Chancellor of the Exchequer despite the heavy administrative burden on a man now seventy years old. The result was collapse, and the illness was put down to overwork. The shadow of 1874 is also seen in plans for reform of rating and the land laws. Of the displaced leaders, Granville had returned to the Foreign Office and Hartington had gone to the India Office. It was said at the time, and historians agree, that had Hartington made the Government he would have been obliged to slant it towards the Radicals. Gladstone could afford to slant it towards the Whigs. Childers became Secretary of State for War, Kimberley for the Colonies; Northbrook, who had been Liberal Viceroy of India, went to the Admiralty; Spencer was Lord President of the Council with responsibility for education; Sir William Harcourt, an angular man and critic of Gladstone but no Radical, went to the Home Office; Selborne, a good Lord Chancellor, was made Chancellor again; W.E. Forster became Chief Secretary for Ireland with a weak viceroy, Lord Cowper. Of the three who looked like Radicals, John Bright as Chancellor for the Duchy of Lancaster, and not truly therefore a departmental minister, was ill and old, J.G. Dodson at the Local Government Board was an intellectual rather than political Radical, so that only Joseph Chamberlain at the Board of Trade, and inclined to think himself underrated, truly represented the Radical wing of the party.

Gladstone's relationship with Chamberlain (see p. 106) mingled instinctive distaste with admiration for his ability. 'He is a man worth watching and studying', he wrote to Granville, 'I should think of great tenacity of purpose: expecting to play an historical part, and probably destined to it.'[54] He had accepted Chamberlain's invitation to address the meeting at Birmingham on 31 May 1877 of delegates from local Liberal associations to inaugurate the National Liberal Federation. He had spoken to 2,500 people, being careful to limit himself to his attack on Beaconsfield's Eastern policy and to guard himself against being supposed to approve of an attempt to reorganize the national Liberal Party from Birmingham. He was unsympathetic to the rigid organiza-tion of the Birmingham caucus and to Chamberlain's ruthlessness, and found his Unitarianism unacceptable. Gladstone had been shocked by his brother Robertson's marriage with a Unitarian.

Reform of rating and the land laws was soon pushed aside by Ireland. Forster's Compensation for Disturbance Bill which extended the principle enacted in 1870 to all cases of disturbance including disturbance for non-payment of rent, was rejected by the Lords. Forster then yielded to the temptation to solve the Irish problem by force and repression. In the summer and autumn of 1880 others − Chamberlain, Bright, Childers and Gladstone himself − were canvassing radical solutions. Chamberlain thought in terms of capital investment. He would pour public money into various economic schemes and advance money to enable farmers to buy their farms. Gladstone accepted land purchase if it was combined with the degree of self-government he was already prepared to admit in Ireland. He wanted elected Irish County Boards to run an extended scheme of land purchase: a memorandum of October showed how far he was prepared to go. The failure of all schemes such as these in the Cabinet caused concentration of effort on a new land bill. Its basis was fair rent, free sale (i.e. of the tenant's right in his land) and fixed tenure, and its terms were influenced by the report of the Bessborough Commission. It was worked through the Cabinet in December and in draft in January 1881. Meanwhile Forster, backed by Cowper, who seems to have lost his nerve, was pleading for coercion and Gladstone was arguing as usual against it. 'With regard to the suspension of the Habeas Corpus Act,' he wrote on 25 October, 'I look to it with feelings not only of aversion on general grounds, but of doubt and much misgiving as to the likelihood of its proving efficacious in the particular case.' It would not stop the fiery language that was the real incitement to violence. Both Forster and Chamberlain threatened resignation, one if coercion were refused, the other if it were granted. Spencer on 22 November gave his support to Forster and others followed.[55] The Cabinet decided against Gladstone and in the last days of December he yielded. The Cabinet had decided that 'coercion was to precede remedy'. It was the condition on which it would accept a good land bill. This bargain ensured the passing of the Land Act in 1881 but prevented the revival of any measure of radical reform, including schemes for widening local responsibilities. So the Irish problem was not solved and in the future Ireland would be the all-absorbing question. The way began to point forward to Home Rule and the break-up of the Liberal Party.

Gladstone's second Midlothian campaign in March 1880 had denounced Beaconsfield's foreign policy, but already on 5 April he published an address to the electors of Midlothian announcing that he 'proposed to desist from any further reference to the indictment' of the proceedings of the Government.[56] He said he did it so as to escape quietly back to Hawarden, but it was really an indication of the change that prospect of office meant. Britain was committed by the Treaty of Berlin and the Cyprus Convention. He might denounce them in opposition but in office he would accept them. Some months later, the Queen protested against what she misunderstood as a reversal of Disraeli's Turkish policy. She was told there had been no reversal. Gladstone wrote in the same month:

> Those of us who sit in the House of Commons . . . were certainly not returned to Parliament to carry forward the Foreign Policy of the last Government. And this was known throughout the country, and beyond it. Nevertheless, sensible of the expediency of maintaining as far as might be a continuity in Foreign Policy, we sought for a ground of action that might be common to both political parties. We found this ground in the unfulfilled Clauses of the Treaty of Berlin.[57]

So on 2 May Gladstone had sent to his Foreign Secretary a draft of a circular despatch to be sent to all five European Powers proposing that they should summon Turkey to fulfil these clauses. They were in fact two: one relating to cession of access to the sea to the new independent state of Montenegro, which had been fixed by much tedious negotiation while the Tories were still in office as an area including Dulcigno; the other was an extension of Greece northwards to include Janina fixed by a decision of a conference in Berlin in June 1880. Goschen, instead of taking a Cabinet post, went on a special embassy to Turkey to obtain the execution of the treaty. It is surprising how near to measures of force Gladstone came in the pressure upon Turkey which followed. It is equally to be noticed that it was not isolated British action, but action by the European Powers in concert, of which he was the mainspring throughout 1880. The Montenegrin question was settled on 9 October when Turkey announced a formal reply to the European Powers agreeing to the cession prescribed. Turkey agreed under the false impression that Britain was about to seize Smyrna. A European fleet (four ships each from Britain and Austria, two each from Italy and Russia, one from Germany and three from France) under the command of Admiral Seymour had been off Ragusa since 14 September. The naval demonstration did not seem a particularly appropriate measure for its purpose and had not frightened the Turks. But Gladstone's enquiries about the strength of Preversa,

Salonika and Smyrna had produced preparations of a sort in the Admiralty and much newspaper speculation and rumour. *The Pall Mall Gazette* announced the intention to occupy Smyrna. Turkey yielded on 10 October. Three days later Gladstone was already pressing Granville to go on to the Greek cession.[58] In April 1881 Gladstone renewed his enquiries about possible measures of force.[59] Turkey again yielded – perhaps because much wider cessions were being canvassed, including the cession of Crete. A Graeco-Turkish Convention signed under the united pressure of the European Powers on 24 May concluded this question. Gladstone had been the mainspring of British policy and European action.

There remained yet another element in Tory foreign policy which in the second Midlothian campaign Gladstone seemed to have committed the Liberals to reverse. He had denounced the occupation of Cyprus under the Anglo-Turkish Convention of 4 June 1878. By this, the occupation was justified by a promise of British assistance to defend Turkey in Asia. But this promise in turn was conditional on the reform of Turkish government in her Asiatic provinces. Instructions to Goschen were drafted which did not propose the evacuation of Cyprus. Gladstone had thought of a more ingenious idea: Goschen was to propose to the Sultan that Britain should buy 'the fee-simple' of Cyprus and the abrogation of the Convention. The instructions were not sent. The stumbling block was the Armenians. If the Convention was abandoned then the Sultan's promise of reform would also be abandoned and an improvement in the conditions of the Armenians, which article 61 of the Treaty of Berlin also committed Britain to obtain, would only rest 'upon such general rights as belong to civilised Powers to take cognisance in extreme cases of misgovernment & misery'. Cyprus remained in British occupation, though its revenues were used to pay the interest due to Britain on a loan to Turkey who remained sovereign of Cyprus. Goschen continued, until his mission ended in June 1881, to press Turkey to reform and thus to cause, as a result, a deterioration in Anglo-Turkish relations. The small discontinuity in British foreign policy in 1880 was a solemn warning to the Turkish ambassador administered by Gladstone after consultation with Granville on 14 May 1880 that Turkey should not base her policy on an expectation of British aid 'in the last resort'.[60] Yet the whole point of the election as Gladstone had fought it had been the overthrow of 'Beaconsfieldism'. Such was Gladstone's realism, his habit of approximating to the ideal, of adapting ideal solutions to existing circumstances.

Early in life (1844) Gladstone agreed with his wife to live on the income from their inherited wealth, to pass the inheritance to their children and to 'give what we earn or save'.[61] His retirement was marked by an attempt to get rid of wealth. He handed over ownership of the Hawarden estate to his eldest son; his collection of china and 11 Carlton House Terrace were both sold. Indicative of the national position he commanded by 1880 was the extraordinary burden of his correspondence – letters were answered, without the help of secretarial assistance, except from children during 1874–80 – reaching a rough maximum of four hundred letters a day and a rare minimum of thirty.

4

The End of Gladstonian Liberalism:
Irish Home Rule

1881–1898

The previous chapter showed how Gladstone returned as Prime Minister with a backward look to 1874 but found it impossible to pick up the legislative or policy threads of the first administration and was directed by events towards Ireland. After his return from a tour of country houses in Ireland in 1877 he had written to Granville: 'Had the Home Rulers a real leader whom they were disposed to follow I cannot think it would be difficult to arrange a *modus vivendi* with them'. He did not suppose that anything more than a compromise with the Home Rulers was attainable though he clearly considered a radical possibility. 'I go much further than the "average" Liberal'. What he had in mind was 'Local Government'. In the second Midlothian speech two years later he said 'I will consent to give to Ireland no principle, nothing that is not upon equal terms offered to Scotland and to the different portions of the United Kingdom'. Business should be 'devolved' from the Westminster Parliament on to County Boards (County Councils did not exist until 1889) in Scotland, England, Wales and Ireland: local government all round.[1] He had embodied this solution for Ireland in a memorandum of 23 October 1880 (see p. 56), rejected by the Cabinet in a succession of meetings in November.[2] This was Gladstone's ideal solution. Because he could not achieve it, he acted increasingly by yielding to pressure: pressure from 'a real leader' who had emerged. Charles Stewart Parnell was recruited to the Land League by Michael Davitt who succeeded the gentle Isaac Butt in 1879. Parnell was an Irish landowner of English Protestant descent with a hatred of England, formulated in the language of the American War of Independence by an American mother. He had no respect at all for the practices of the House of Commons, where he first sat in 1875. His chief instrument of action at Westminster was a calculated campaign of obstruction – a serious obstacle to co-operation with Gladstone. In Ireland it was to be the National League, founded in October 1882.

The year 1881 began for Gladstone without that pause for reflection that his birthday and New Year's eve generally gave him. The Cabinet met on both 30 and 31 December. 'This year', he wrote, 'I have been quite unable to recover and extricate my mind from cares of Government and of the state of Ireland in particular'.[3] The new session began on 7 January 1881. He faced it as Chancellor of the Exchequer, with the task of carrying through the House a budget based on the unattractive principle of watching expenditure and keeping it low rather than watching the revenue and keeping it high; as leader of the House of Commons with the prospect of an Affirmation Bill for Bradlaugh, the atheist, elected MP for Northampton but not allowed to take his seat in 1880 either when he tried to affirm or when he tried to take the oath; as Prime Minister with the task of bringing the Cabinet to agree on the Transvaal where the Boers had risen against the annexation effected by the Beaconsfield Government in 1877. Gladstone in Midlothian had denounced its South African policy, but his Government had not reversed it nor recalled Sir Bartle Frere, the main instigator of it, until July. Now during January and February 1881 a tiny British force advancing towards the Transvaal from Natal was to be defeated twice, and then a third time at Majuba Hill (27 February). Worst of all was the Irish prospect. Gladstone was committed to a policy of 'coercion before remedy', to which he (and Chamberlain) had a deep aversion and in whose success he and others had no confidence. Overshadowing all was the knowledge that Commons procedure would be thrown into chaos by the tactics of the Irish members.

At least the Irish bills had been prepared. The first coercion bill, the Life and Property Protection Bill, which gave the viceroy temporary power to arrest and imprison anyone without trial in proclaimed districts, was introduced by Forster on 27 January. On 31 January the House sat for twenty-four hours continuously. Gladstone made an effort to force the bill through its first stage, but was defeated by the ingenuity of the Irish opposition. The Speaker then sent for Gladstone and said he would close the debate on his own authority after a delay till the next morning, provided Gladstone, as leader of the House, would propose some regulation of procedure. Thus the bill got through its first stage and, since the House passed Gladstone's resolutions on procedure, was assured of enactment. By the reform of procedure the

Speaker was given power to close a debate if a ministerial motion that its subject was urgent was passed by a majority of 3 to 1. Gladstone's speech (3 February) was one of his finest. Forster then introduced the second coercion bill (1 March). The Peace Preservation (Ireland) Bill, regulating the carrying and possession of arms, violated Gladstone's primary principle of allowing nothing for Ireland that was not equally for the other parts of the British Isles. By using the urgency resolution the bill was enacted on 21 March.

Gladstone was next preoccupied with his budget. His speech introducing it was something of a triumph and the Government seemed to recover. Then on 7 April he introduced the Irish land bill. Next day Argyll resigned, unable to share responsibility for legislation he opposed. His resignation was not unexpected. Granville and Spencer tried to persuade him to stay but in vain. The fouth bill for Ireland promised in the Queen's Speech, a bill for 'the establishment of County Government in Ireland, founded upon the representative principle with the aims of extending popular control over expenditure and the formation of habits of local self-government', was never introduced. The land bill took fifty-eight sittings to pass. It was longer in committe than even the second reform bill. When finally enacted it gave the Irish tenant farmers 'the three Fs' − fair rents (fixed by judicial tribunals for fifteen years on the application of either tenant or landowner); fixity of tenure by restricting the landlord's power of eviction; and free sale of his interest in the land. It extended the state's share of help to the tenant buying his farm under the Bright clause of the 1870 act. It was to prove to be far from a settlement. It failed to deal with the grievances of some 150,000 leaseholders. Some 130,000 tenants could not take advantage of it because they were in arrears with their rent. The provisions for land purchase were still inadequate. Another portent was that the bill had raised yet again the conflict with the Tory majority in the House of Lords. All that can be said is that the act of 1881 was a better act than that of 1870. Yet the session had proved once again Gladstone's great ability, not with individuals − Argyll had gone, Chamberlain was unreconciled − but with the House of Commons. Hartington said on 6 August, and it has been often quoted, 'the history of the last seven months is the record of energy and resolution, the knowledge and the resource of one man'.[4]

Gladstone had worked too little with Chamberlain, the only member of the Cabinet who really shared his views about local self-government, and he made no attempt to overcome the mutual mistrust that existed between himself and Parnell. When Parnell now recommended tenants to go warily in accepting the land act (in September a number of test cases were brought before the tribunals), his advice was interpreted as an effort to wreck its execution.

The autumn of 1881 was disastrous in Ireland. Outrages increased from 769 for January to March to 1,060 for July to September.[5] A contributory cause was the ineptitude of the Irish executive. Gladstone persuaded Spencer to return to Ireland as viceroy but he only went back on 6 May – a momentous day. Forster was worn out by his struggles in the Cabinet and House of Commons over coercion, while his schemes to improve police protection broke down. When coercion failed, his answer was more repression, and here he met again the opposition of Gladstone and Chamberlain. He was replaced by Lord Frederick Cavendish in May 1882. Meanwhile Gladstone had drawn the conclusion from the small Home Rule vote in the Tyrone by-election of September 1881 that Parnell's following was less to be dealt with than Parnell himself.[6] He was confirmed in his conviction that Irish local self-government was the next step and at Leeds (7 October) warned Parnell that the 'resources of civilisation against its enemies are not yet exhausted'. Granville had held him back from far-reaching commitment to 'Home or local rule' and he had limited himself to a general affirmation of the supremacy of the imperial Parliament.[7] But his thoughts were now irrevocably fixed on the isolation of Parnell and legislation for Irish local government. Parnell answered Gladstone's speech at Leeds with defiance at Wexford and on 12 October 1881 the Cabinet – in a meeting of five instead of the normal two or three hours – decided to arrest and imprison Parnell. It seemed to be vindicated when, in November, tenants began to flock to the Land Courts.

Gladstone was now preoccupied with local government and rating, and with the legislative programme for 1882. Besides bills on English local government, and London government, there was to be a bill to set up four elective Provincial Councils in Ireland, an effective land purchase bill (one third of the purchase money to be provided by the State, one third by the landlord and one third by the tenant) administered by the new Councils, and an Arrears Bill to release tenants from accumulated arrears of rent. The programme even included the budget, since reform of local government, including Irish local government, would transfer costs from central to local authorities, and so enable the Chancellor further to reduce taxation.[8] But the whole programme, both English and Irish, except for the Arrears Bill, had to be abandoned. The year 1882 was legislatively barren.

Meanwhile, with this programme of real solutions in mind, the Government began to relax coercion. Parnell was released from Kilmainham gaol with the understanding contained in a letter to Captain O'Shea, that 'the exertions we [i.e. Parnell and his colleagues] should be able to make strenuously and unremittingly would be effective in stopping outrage and intimidation of all kinds'.[9] The O'Shea connection was disastrous, not only because O'Shea was not single-minded, but also because Mrs O'Shea, Parnell's mistress, took advantage of it to begin a correspondence with Gladstone which introduced a muddling element into his notions of what he could do by co-operating with Parnell. Gladstone knew of the relationship because Granville had written of it to him but he tended to ignore it, treating Mrs O'Shea with aloof courtesy.[10] She was, after all, sister to Sir Evelyn Wood and niece to the Lord Chancellor of his first administration. Parnell was released on 2 May. The policy of relaxed coercion lasted just four days. On 6 May the new Chief Secretary, Lord Frederick Cavendish, and the Under Secretary, T.H. Burke, were murdered as they walked home through Phoenix Park. Cavendish was married to Mrs Gladstone's niece and had been Gladstone's private secretary. It was a personal blow from which he may never have recovered. On 8 May he went to the House of Commons and 'by the help of God spoke out what was needful', but the tragedy increased rather than allayed bitterness. It may have had something to do with the final implacability of Gladstone's resolve to give Ireland a separate parliament.

The year 1882 was also the year of the British occupation of Egypt. That this should have been the work of a Prime Minister so opposed to the occupation of Cyprus in 1878, as his Midlothian speeches of March 1880 had shown him, needs some explanation – particularly since in the Convention of Pretoria of August 1881, which had given the Transvaal qualified independence, he had so recently appeared true to anti-Beaconsfieldism. The end of the Anglo-French control of Egypt was certainly a departure from Tory policy, but since it eventuated in military operations in Egypt and then war in the Sudan against the Mahdi, it looked more like doing what the Tories did, only doing it worse. The policy had not been designed but grew out of a revolutionary situation in Egypt, arising out of wholly Egyptian circumstances, out of diplomatic responses in Paris and Cairo to British initiatives and eventually out of responses to action by Admiral Seymour in 1882 and by General Gordon in 1884.[11]

The starting-point of the Egyptian story is the debt incurred by the Egyptian ruler to foreign bondholders, chiefly, but not exclusively, French and British. Three successive financial crises in less than three years, when the Khedive was unable to pay the interest due, brought Egypt under tighter and tighter foreign control. The revenues assigned to the payment of interest went into an internationally controlled *Caisse de la Dette publique;* foreigners filled more and more of the posts in public administration; by the last arrangement of November 1879 two Controllers-General, one appointed by the French and one by the British Government, administered Egyptian finances, the French in charge of revenue and the British in charge of expenditure. This distribution of functions was a pointer to a growing inequality between the French and the British influence and the French diplomatic representative already reported that there was no *'égalité de situation entre les deux pays'.*[12] An international Commission of Liquidation was also at work and produced a law of liquidation by 1880. Its indebtedness thus brought Egypt, an agrarian, Muslim country of oppressed peasants and powerful landowners, into the Christian European world of economic capitalism and alien ideas of administration and justice. Out of this grew a revolutionary situation of a classic kind: on one side, the Khedive's government, and beyond it his Turkish sovereign, losing authority and finding its army, with more than half its officers on half pay and its soldiers unpaid, aggrieved and in revolt; on the other side a peasantry, grown prosperous as foreign administration brought regular taxation and known, fixed obligations, conceiving new possibilities, while landowners, whether sheikhs in the villages or their delegates in the Chamber of Notables, were coalescing with army and religious leaders against both Khedive and foreigner. There was a vacuum of power in Egypt which neither the leader of the 'national' movement, such as it was, Colonel Arabi, nor the Chamber of Notables was ready to fill. Riots in Alexandria and the presence of an Anglo-French fleet in the Roads were the result of this situation. The minister now in power in France was working a policy which he took from the Chamber of Deputies. When the Chamber refused him the necessary credits for the naval protection of the Suez Canal he withdrew the French ships. This left Admiral Seymour to stay to be defied by the Egyptians under Arabi, whom he summoned to surrender the forts which Arabi had been busily arming, with their guns trained on the Anglo-French fleet.

Gladstone believed his Government was bound by the agreements concluded by the Tory Foreign Secretary, Salisbury, in September 1878.

These were informal and secret, taking the shape of an exchange of despatches which looked to British acquiescence in a French occupation of Tunis, a British occupation of Cyprus and equal partnership in Egypt. But by September 1882 he wrote 'There is nothing I think more clear in the Egyptian matter than that the *dual action* must be abolished'.[13] He had reached this conclusion by a series of most characteristic moves. He had first believed that Turkey as the legal sovereign should be induced to send troops to Egypt and Turkey had, in fact, sent two ineffectual emissaries in October 1881 and a grander but still ineffectual mission in June 1882. He had next attempted to bring about European action. 'Should you be very averse', he asked Granville, 'to extending the Anglo-French concert in Egypt to an European concert?'[14] But nothing came of this except a conference of ambassadors in session at the Turkish capital, 23 June to 14 August. Finally, he had been most uncomfortable about Seymour's summons to Arabi. Since Britain had no sovereign rights in Egypt he could not demand the 'surrender' of the forts. Gladstone insisted by telegram on an alteration in the wording of the summons; surrender was to be changed to 'surrender for dismantling'. It had no effect on the sequence of events. On 3 July Seymour was instructed, after his summons to Arabi, to silence the guns. Seymour summoned Arabi to surrender the forts and so practically committed his Government to take power out of Arabi's hands into its own. On 11 July he bombarded the forts. On 12 July fire broke out and the town was pillaged. Seymour telegraphed for two battalions from Cyprus. On 15 July the town was policed by 800 British soldiers, Arabi's forces having withdrawn into the interior. On 17 July, Seymour in a proclamation posted in Alexandria announced that 'with the permission of the Khedive' he alone was responsible for maintaining order. He had fully committed his Government. On 14 July the House of Commons voted the credits for the military occupation of Egypt and the protection of the Suez Canal. It was a fortnight after the bombardment before troops arrived in Egypt sufficient to occupy it. Troops came from Malta and Gibraltar on 25 to 27 July. General Wolseley only arrived from Britain with the main British force on 4 August. On 13 September the Battle of Tel-el-Kebir made the British the only effective army in Egypt. Thus when the Sudan revolted, it was that army which went to pacify it. Gladstone, to the Queen's annoyance, wanted early evacuation. But his wishes were in vain and British troops were to remain in Egypt until 1956.

Gladstone and Granville ended by incurring the hostility of Germany over its colonial development as well as the hostility of France over Egypt, and nearly came to war with Russia over its expansion in Turkestan to the Afghan frontier. Gladstone's attempt to base foreign policy upon general European opinion of what was right was unsuitable to a situation which was governed, as long as Bismarck prevailed, by power politics. Bismarck had three complaints against Britain. Gladstone and Granville took, he said, an obstructive attitude. Having long established colonies itself, Britain meant to monopolize the colonial field. Secondly, Granville, he said, had handled a perfectly legitimate question from Germany, whether Britain would protect German settlers in what became German South West Africa (and is now Namibia), with insolent neglect. The explanation was not insolence but misunderstanding. Granville believed Bismarck was opposed to German colonial development as he had always said he was and thought he was inviting the answer 'no' from Britain, the ruler of South Africa, an answer which he could then use at home against German shippers and commercial interests clamouring for colonial development. Thirdly, in a certain despatch, dated 5 May 1884, and addressed to the German ambassador in London, Bismarck had hinted at the cession of Heligoland by Britain to Germany as part of a general colonial bargain. No reply was ever made to this. At the time it was said that Münster had failed to communicate its contents, but a letter from Granville to Gladstone, 28 December 1884, discusses a possible reply to the request for Heligoland.[15] It was, however, never sent so that part of Bismarck's accusation was fair. But Gladstone and Granville may have been practising a prudent silence rather than a high-handed arrogance. Anyhow, between spring 1884 and spring 1885 Germany founded her colonies of Togoland, Kamerun, South West and South East Africa and at the Berlin West Africa Conference in November 1884 there seemed to be a Franco-German *entente* directed against Britain. Germany was also the inspirer of the European opposition which compelled Britain to abandon a treaty with Portugal recognizing Portuguese sovereignty at the mouth of the Congo, an extension of Portuguese Angola long claimed.

The Liberals had opened, it was hoped, a new phase of foreign policy by a characteristically Gladstonian attempt in April 1880 to establish a better relationship with Russia. The basis of this improvement was to be a British accommodation to Russian policy in Turkestan. The consequence of this was not improved relations, but a new momentum behind Russia's advance towards the Afghan frontier. By 1884 Russia had occupied all the fair-towns up to territory claimed by Afghanistan.

The difficulty was that there existed among a partially nomadic people no defined frontier as Europeans understood frontiers. Britain agreed with Russia that an Anglo-Russian mission should map and mark out an agreed frontier on the ground. The British commissioner with a small military escort arrived on the spot but the Russian commissioner delayed his arrival. Meanwhile the Russian occupation forces continued their advance towards mountain passes of strategic importance. The inevitable outcome was a military clash between Russians and Afghans under the eyes of the British troops at Penjdeh on 20 March 1885. Since the Afghans were under the influence of British India and had accepted advice from Britain, a period of acute Anglo-Russian tension from 21 March to 11 May 1885 followed. On 21 March, with a local decision to forestall a Russian seizure, Britain occupied Port Hamilton off South Korea. The crisis was turned by an agreement that neither Afghans nor Russians would advance further until the frontier was fully determined. But the Russians had secured the strategic frontier they wished to have and Britain had abandoned the Turkomans and Afghans to them. Kimberley at the India Office and Northbrook at the Admiralty, but speaking as a former Viceroy of India, wished to support the Afghans but got no help from Gladstone in the Cabinet, and since it was now too late to oppose Russia without risk of war, Gladstone had the majority of the Cabinet with him. He had not understood the force behind Russia's expansionist policy nor that 'European right' as far as Russia was concerned had nothing to do with the case. His activity was directed to parrying Tory questions in the House of Commons and providing the evasions and distinctions which allowed the final settlement to be made.[16]

To understand how seriously the Government was under political pressure by 1885 we must return to 1882 and the Irish question. The Government had been badly damaged in the spring of 1882 by the debates on the so-called Kilmainham treaty. Gladstone insisted that there was no treaty, only a *transaction* in the French sense. It was a narrow distinction, not widely adopted. It had been further damaged by Forster's speeches explaining his resignation, by Balfour's biting tongue in the Commons and Salisbury's cold disdain in the Lords. Further offers from Parnell in June and October the Cabinet decided to repel. It went ahead with stiffer coercion. Harcourt introduced the Prevention of Crimes (Ireland) Bill and Spencer reorganized the Irish police. It is true the bill withdrew the power of arbitrary imprisonment from the viceroy, but the provision now made for dealing with outrages included punishment for incitement to violence in speech or writing, and powers to suppress newspapers. Aimed at the secret societies, it suppressed trial by jury in certain cases. All Gladstone's attempts to soften his own Government's bill, by withdrawing for example its provision for searching houses, were defeated.

The one success of the Government in 1882 was its Arrears Bill, introduced on 15 May. It encountered the resistance of the House of Lords where the Irish landlord interest was strong. The Lords only passed the bill at the end of July on Gladstone's threatening a dissolution. The Arrears Act was a success in Ireland and much facilitated the working of the 1881 Land Act. Arrears were no longer a barrier to using the Land Courts and judicial rents were being fixed all over the country. The autumn of 1882 was devoted to an autumn session of Parliament, and to more reform of parliamentary procedure. Further rules for regulating debate were adopted. Two permanent Grand Committees (which Gladstone had proposed in 1871, see p. 69) were up, one for legal and one for commercial business. These Chamberlain used in 1883 to consolidate and reform bankruptcy law and patent law while the Chancellor used them to enact legal reform, avoiding the normal committee stage when bills were considered by a committee of the whole House.

Gladstone, who had already collapsed in 1880 and had been away from July to September 1882, was exhausted. He wrote on 24 October 1882 to Spencer, summing up and expanding a conversation they had had at Hawarden. He proposed to retire before the end of the parliamentary session, because he had done for Ireland what he could and had reformed procedure, because of his old age and his increasing disinclination to his work. The letter was sent to Granville and to Hartington. Granville replied:

> Your case is not normal. Your bodily and mental strength are exceptionally strong. What young or middle aged man possesses in an equal degree the capacity which you describe as necessary for a prime minister and which you are afraid may fail you. The hold you have on the country is extraordinary. The power you possess to confer exceptional advantages on it, is exceptional.

The letter was well expressed to persuade him to stay. On 11 November Gladstone renewed his proposal averring that Granville's letter had not touched 'my central and conclusive reason, which is inability, inability of brain, to face the legislative work that must come on'.[17] On

8 December *The Times* published a leading article announcing as likely Gladstone's resignation as Chancellor of the Exchequer, his replacement by Childers and the accession to the Cabinet of Derby and Dilke. This was all that happened. Derby came into the Cabinet as Colonial Secretary and Dilke as President of the Local Government Board. The Queen at once objected since she believed Derby had seriously hampered Beaconsfield whose Foreign Secretary he had been until 1878, and she knew Dilke had publicly professed republicanism. She needed reassurances that he no longer held these opinions. But Dilke was difficult and the Queen determined, though in the end she was the most reasonable of them all. The problem of Gladstone's exhaustion was not solved by his giving up the Exchequer. So he took medical advice, gave up a proposed visit to Midlothian, with the usual speeches and crowded meetings, and on 17 January 1883 went off with his wife and his son Stephen to Cannes. He planned at first to stay until the beginning of the session on 15 February but in the end, with the encouragement of the Queen (she had indeed proposed a peerage in order to lighten his load of work) and his colleagues, stayed until 5 March when he returned to face an Opposition question in the House of Commons on 'the Kilmainham Treaty'.

It is from this long absence, that may be dated the disintegration of Gladstone's second Cabinet. The cabinet was, of course, the mainspring of government and upon his management of his cabinet ultimately depends any prime minister's capacity to make and keep a government. Presiding over his cabinet he helped that approximation of minds which alone justified anyone in calling foreign, defence, colonial or Indian policy the policy of the government. Gladstone found himself in 1883 doing more and more of this work by letter and avoiding actual meetings. Secondly, in finance, however much freedom a Chancellor of the Exchequer might claim or enjoy, his proposals had to be approved in the end and made into government proposals before being brought to the Commons. Gladstone had ceased to fight on this front in 1883 and acceptance of Childers's budget in 1883 was little more than a formality. In its third aspect the Cabinet was programme-maker to Parliament, especially to the Commons. In this aspect it was governed by the parliamentary timetable. The weekly sessional Cabinets and the out-of-session planning Cabinets of the autumn have been mentioned (see p. 59). In the autumn of 1882, Parliament being still in session, the ordinary sessional Cabinets were still meeting. The new session of 1883 seemed likely therefore to begin with no plan. On 3 February

Hartington wrote to Granville, who in Gladstone's absence would cause the Cabinet to be summoned and would preside over it, asking for a meeting and urging him to write to Harcourt 'who is in a fuss about our unprepared condition'. Harcourt wrote himself: 'I am very seriously uneasy at meeting Parliament without any cabinet consultation'. After three further protests Granville held meetings on 6, 9 and 13 February. It was essential at least to have a Queen's Speech, the usual end-result of the planning. Gladstone had done something towards preparing this by letter and the Irish paragraphs had been decided on before he went to Cannes.[18] On 31 January he wrote to Granville on the question of what should be the principal bill for the session. 'Two subjects which have all along been contemplated as belonging to the mission of the present Parliament, are (1) Local Government in Great Britain together with financial changes appertaining to it, and (2) the Representation of the People, in which latter I include Franchise and Redistribution' [i.e. rearrangement of constituencies]. Either of these might be the main bill. 'But I do not feel myself any longer possessed of the mental force necessary to enable me to grapple, in my present position, with subjects of such magnitude and complexity.' He reserved to himself the liberty of retiring 'say, at Easter' if either measure were promised in the Queen's Speech. 'I incline to think however that the Metropolitan Government bill, postponed for 48 years, and embracing the local enfranchisement of four millions of people, *might* suffice for the present year, if combined with other good and practical measures; especially if with a Local Government bill for Ireland.'[19] The preparation of the Queen's Speech limped on. It finally offered local government for Britain beginning with London and proceeding to other areas if time permitted. A list of small measures to begin in the House of Lords was agreed upon and local government for Ireland referred to in general terms. This signalled the beginning of the worst split. Hartington rendered Irish local government impossible by telling his constituents in South East Lancashire on 19 January that 'it would be madness. . .to volunteer to give to Ireland more extended self-government' without assurances from her representatives that it would not be misused.[20]

Harcourt was entrusted with the preparation and introduction of a bill to set up a single municipal council for the whole of London. But he and Gladstone fell into a dispute about the control of the London police. Harcourt was induced to postpone his bill until the Affirmation Bill had been passed. This was a second attempt to get what Gladstone had failed to get in 1881 and 1882. Bradlaugh had continued to try to take the oath and had been expelled whenever he did so. His constituents simply re-elected him. The Government then opened the session in 1883 with a bill to amend the parliamentary oath and allow affirmation. The bill ran a protracted course in the Commons being fought by the Opposition by every device they could contrive, and was defeated by three votes in May. Meanwhile the Cabinet had approved the budget but meetings had been intermitted more than once in March and April. Gladstone's argument with Harcourt continued. Gladstone sought a compromise giving the control of the police to the Municipality as he believed it should be given, but allowing the Crown (i.e. the government of the day) to decide when that clause of the bill should be carried out. Harcourt still insisted that the control should belong to the Home Secretary and did not moderate the strength with which he expressed his views. The dispute had been leaked to the press and the suspicion arose that Harcourt was using Chamberlain's tactic of 'pressure from without'. By the end of May Harcourt saw that it was too late in the session to hope to get his bill through and, with Cabinet assent, abandoned it. It was never introduced.

On 13 June Chamberlain made a speech at Birmingham calling for a new extension of the franchise and other parliamentary reforms. This began a new Cabinet row that reached its climax in November–December 1883 with Chamberlain taking a public stand on the Irish being included in any widening of the franchise, and Hartington taking an equally public stand on their exclusion. No Cabinet meetings were held from 8 to 21 August and the session ended with yet another argument between Lords and Commons when the Lords amended the Agricultural Holdings Bill and the Commons refused to accept the changes. Gladstone's only contribution in this session was to move the grants to be made to Lord Alcester (formerly Admiral Seymour) and Lord Wolseley in recognition of their Egyptian services. From 8 to 20 September 1883 Gladstone was again out of the country, cruising in Scottish and Norwegian waters with Tennyson as companion. There were no Cabinets between 22 August and 25 October. On 22 October Gladstone wrote to Hartington a letter, sent in copy to Granville who was not unprepared for it, in preparation for the Cabinet and to avoid acrimony at the meeting. Since his 'mental force' was unequal to any 'very grave and complex constructive measures' he proposed that the legislative programme for 1884 should be limited to franchise reform, leaving open the extension of household suffrage to Ireland and leaving half the session for local government reform. Gladstone argued with

Hartington by letter and at a series of Cabinet meetings from 10 to 22 November, after which Hartington, still unconvinced, began to hint at resignation and the question whether there were to be separate franchise and redistribution bills was still unsettled. Gladstone did not summon the Cabinet again until 3 January 1884. The dispute came fully into the open when Chamberlain spoke at Bristol and Wolverhampton, insisting on the separation of franchise reform and redistribution and on the lowering of the Irish franchise, and when Hartington at Manchester and Accrington argued that franchise and redistribution must be taken together and Ireland excluded. Thus Gladstone took his Cabinet not only ill-prepared into the session of 1884, but divided into its Whig and Radical wings.

Besides losing his grip on his Cabinet during 1883 Gladstone also lost his hold on his parliamentary following, much in the same way as he lost it during the 1868–74 administration and for much the same reasons. Again, two apparently incompatible things happened simultaneously. There was less and less legislation and more and more bills. There were Chamberlain's successes, the Chancellor's acts already mentioned and Harcourt's Agricultural Holdings Act – but there was no legislative centrepiece. The timetable was increasingly cluttered with bills sanctioning Provisional Orders under General Acts, consolidating bills from the Departments, or little Irish bills promoted by the obstructive Irish members, or a number of bills promoted by the Temperence interest. A reform which enforced the grouping of notices of bills on the first day of the session, instead of each being taken separately in turn before its first reading, saved time, but Parliament was more hard worked than ever and fewer and fewer bills were enacted. Neither the curbing of obstruction nor the setting up of Grand Committees had solved the problem of bill congestion. On 9 May 1883 William Rathbone, a Liverpool merchant and philanthropist, a back-bencher enjoying great respect in the House, wrote to Gladstone describing the discontent of the party and deploring the growing incoherence of parliamentary proceedings. He believed the party was falling apart because the labours of the House were so barren of result and he appealed to Gladstone to call the party together. Gladstone could always recover the enthusiasm of his following with one great speech but he could not hold it any longer for the day-by-day steady plod. Gladstone's solution was not a party meeting which he would only have addressed and not 'managed', but to rely on 'some one measure to rouse and rally the party'.[21] And this as we have seen he was denied in 1883 by the inability of the Cabinet to agree on the Government of London bill. In 1884–85 he tried with parliamentary reform but he did not reunite the disintegrating Cabinet and party.

Another incurable trouble was the defection of Liberal peers to the Tories. Some, including the Duke of Bedford, had gone over on account of the Compensation for Disturbance Bill of 1880. More 'migrations' occurred on the Irish land bill in 1881 and others again when the Lords carried a motion for an enquiry into the working of the land act. Gladstone was opposed to a lavish creation of peers which would bring on a battle with the Queen and which in any case gave no security of future party loyalty. His device of using household office to attract young peers to political activity by giving each officeholder the duty of representing some department in the Lords was of very limited effect. He used it with Lansdowne, and Lansdowne defected. Granville had to manage an ever-diminishing following and was to have considerable difficulty in finding enough peers to fill the household offices when Gladstone made his third Government.

Meanwhile, on 3 January 1884 Hartington agreed gracefully to the introduction of a separate franchise bill and that the Irish should be included in it on the same terms as the rest of the British Isles. On the following day the Cabinet adopted the franchise bill to 'the general satisfaction', Gladstone going out of his way to restrain Chamberlain and to consult Hartington. The franchise bill, equalizing the county with the existing borough franchise, was then drafted and between 22 January and 6 February the Cabinet went through it clause by clause. Cabinet cohesion was better under the first impact of the Sudan crisis, but the improvement did not last. On 28 February Gladstone introduced the franchise bill. Then from 10 to 31 March he was again first ill and then convalescent outside London. Granville was again presiding over Cabinets. Thus Gladstone was absent − against his intentions − on the first night of the second reading of the bill (24 March). He attended the House to defend General Gordon's mission on 4 April but was soon absent again, staying with Rosebery at the Durdans near Epsom from 8 to 15 April and then going on to Granville's brother at Holmbury, where Granville was also staying − this was of course convenient for the foreign crises of these days. On 12 May Gladstone made his great speech referring to the Sudanese as 'a people rightly struggling to be free', carrying more than the Liberal members' admiration and enthusiasm with him but, as so often, fewer mens' second thoughts. It was not until 23 May that he began seriously to help Hartington in working the franchise bill through the House. The committee and report stages dragged on so that it was not until 26 June that it passed the Commons. The bill now went to the Lords where its failure was near certain. Nor did Granville and Gladstone, by writing (4 July) respectively to peers in embassies and other foreign posts and to the bishops begging them to come to London to vote, much improve its chances. During its second reading Granville made, through Cairns, the Government's final offer to Salisbury, the leader of the Tory Opposition. He gave an assurance that there would be no general election on the new franchise in the old constituencies, that is before a redistribution bill. This Salisbury declined and the Lords shelved the bill. It was a government defeat, but Gladstone took the decision 'not to dissolve at the dictation of the Lords' and defended the decision at a party meeting on 10 July. It was a formal occasion addressed by Gladstone, Goschen, who explained his conversion to the franchise bill, and John Bright. It failed to give any real sense of direction to the Liberal back-benchers, its tone being too retrospective.[22]

It was at this point that Gladstone's relations with the Queen became all-important (see p. 45). These had been cool from the beginning of the administration because of his Irish and Egyptian policies. They had warmed a little when he was ill in February 1883 and she had suggested a peerage. Granville was essential in smoothing the request for a prorogation instead of the dissolution, on the understanding that there would be an autumn session and a fresh franchise bill. It was intended that the interval should be spent in finding terms on which the Tory majority in the Lords would pass it. Granville, who was at Osborne from 25 to 27 August, persuaded the Queen to help in avoiding a constitutional crisis. The Queen then invited Gladstone to Balmoral (9–10 September) for the first time during this administration. More important in the end were the visits of the Duke of Richmond there on 12–14 September and again on 13 November. Each side mistrusted the other; the Liberals suspected that the Tories would after all not pass their bills and the Tories that the redistribution bill when it came would work constituency boundaries to the Liberals' advantage. Each side was averse to committing itself first. That assurances were finally given in formulae agreed upon by conferences of Liberal and Tory Lords and the principles of an acceptable redistribution bill worked out owed something to the Queen's intervention as well as to the conciliatory skills of Granville, Cairns, Richmond and Salisbury and to Gladstone's inventiveness. Franchise reform was thus enacted in 1884 and the constituency changes in 1885.

In 1885 the Government was swamped with foreign crises while the Cabinet was more seriously divided than ever over the estimates. The back-benchers were more restive than ever and a further party meeting of December 1884 had been as useless as all previous ones. Gladstone was deluged with letters complaining of the disintegration of the parliamentary party. Samuel Whitbread and Joseph Pease were among these correspondents.[23] Cabinet government began to show fresh signs of collapse. Cabinet meetings were both too few, since Gladstone avoided summoning them whenever he could, and too many, since adjournment from meeting to meeting brought a number in succession when in more harmonious situations one would have sufficed. Failing a real approximation of opinion by candid discussion aimed at agreement, decisions were taken by vote. Matters of first-class importance were decided in small committees.

The decision to send General Gordon to the Sudan was taken by Granville, Hartington, Northbrook and Dilke meeting 'in conclave' in January 1884. Gladstone's agreement was given by telegram after the decision. He was anyhow sent, not as the best man to do the job, but to get the War Office out of 'a mess'. Already in November 1883 Granville was looking for some way of 'using Chinese Gordon', who had made a reputation in Egypt by serving the Khedive in the Sudan in 1874–78. Granville was prompted by Gordon's having lost his rank and pay in the British army because of the misciphering of a War Office telegram. Gordon had asked permission to take service under Stanley in the Congo. A telegram 'the Secretary of State declines to sanction arrangement' was received by Gordon with the word 'decides' instead of 'declines'. He had accepted appointment and was then cashiered for doing so. Hartington repaired the injustice by proposing his mission to the Sudan. He left the same night the decision was taken with carefully safeguarded instructions. He was to 'report on the military situation at Khartoum, on the means to evacuate the interior, to secure the Red Sea coast and to stop the slave trade.'[24] But Gordon was too strong-willed to be content to report. By a series of telegraphic exchanges he altered his mission to an executive one: to withdraw the Egyptian garrisons from the interior. Now in command of a British force in the Sudan he arrived at Khartoum and before evacuating the garrisons, justifiably, concerned himself about what security forces should replace them. In the spring and summer of 1884 the British public, House of Commons and Cabinet were all concerned about whether Gordon should or should not make Zobeir Pasha Governor of Khartoum after he left and use him in evacuating the garrisons. The trouble was that Zobeir was a notorious slave dealer, but Gladstone wished Gordon to use him.[25]

As is well known, Gordon was beleaguered in Khartoum. The question of a relief expedition succeeded the question of Zobeir. The Cabinets of 27 May and 16 July decided, disastrously, against preparations to reinforce or relieve Gordon. There was general support for Hartington, backed by Selborne, who wished to send troops. Indeed, Hartington had from the beginning tried to give Gordon effective strength. Gladstone was alone in wishing both to use Zobeir Pasha and not to reinforce Gordon: for once, he carried his view. He continued obstinately unresponsive to Hartington's and others' strong sense of urgency over the Sudan. The decision taken after three Cabinets in August to ask for a vote of credit for undefined military preparations was a success for Hartington and the Cabinet and a defeat for Gladstone.[26] Gordon and his men were killed at Khartoum on 26 January 1885 and the relief expedition arrived too late. The Sudan had to be reconquered in 1896–98.

The death of Gordon masked the few successes of the Government abroad. The European financial conference over Egypt, the Suez Canal agreement, the settlement with France of a dispute in Madagascar and the work of state building that went on in Egypt under Sir Evelyn Baring and Northbrook, who was sent on a temporary mission, were all successes which made no mark on the public drift away from Gladstone. Less successful in the long term was the Convention of London (1884) which further qualified the independence restored to the Transvaal in 1881, but it at least brought an end to the Boer War, renewed in 1883. The chief mark, after the death of Gordon, was made by the crises with Germany and Russia already described.

Throughout 1884 there were constant redefinitions of Cabinet divisions and inconclusive, adjourned or evaded decisions. Over reducing the British occupying forces in Egypt as over the Sudan, Hartington was on one side and Gladstone on the other. Hartington and Northbrook opposed Gladstone again when he wished to reduce their Departments' estimates. Harcourt and Selborne or Harcourt and Chamberlain with Dilke were regular pairs of disputants. Four Cabinets in November–December 1884 divided on Northbrook's report on

Egyptian finances. 'I hope', Gladstone wrote, 'we shall not have a general discussion on this today for fear of creating difficulties. We should try to adjust among a few of us'. The same letter might have been written before any of the Cabinets of 1885. On 21 April, the first of the three final crises, division opened up on the budget which had to be postponed. The Irish question, a revision of the Crimes Act and land purchase on 6, 9 and especially 15 May, provided the second crisis and could not be settled. The third came when discussion on the budget was resumed on 5 June. On this, after defeat in the Commons, the Government resigned. A stopgap Tory Government came in because the registers were not ready for a general election.

Gladstone was now ill, his voice gone and throat painful and he was thinking of two months' complete rest. His ideas on Ireland evolved in correspondence with Granville, Spencer, Derby and others. His correspondents also consulted together. It was still 'local government' for Ireland that was under discussion. In general terms the writers agreed on this. On the crucial proposal for a 'central board' in Dublin, they divided. Both Granville and Derby made objections to this. Derby wrote, 'The new board meeting in Dublin would be considered by everybody as a local parliament, and would certainly claim to be one'. There would be constant pressure to enlarge its functions until it would be Home Rule with the Irish members still at Westminster. 'I object', he added in a second letter, 'on the ground that in such a board, or council, Ulster will be in a permanent minority. . . We shall begin by alienating the only real friends whom we have in Ireland'.[27] Granville's objections seem to have been similar, made perhaps by word of mouth. At the beginning of August Gladstone had begun to shift away from local government. He wrote to Granville, 'As far as I can learn both you and Derby are on the same lines as Parnell, in rejecting the smaller & repudiating the larger scheme. . . For my own part I have seen my way pretty well as to the particulars of the minor & rejected plan, but the idea of the wider one puzzles me much.'[28] Did he mean by 'the wider one' the central board or a separate parliament? He would seem to be as bewildered as he was bewildering. In this bewilderment Gladstone went off on a sea cruise to Norway with Sir Thomas and Lady Brassey. He did not on this occasion visit Copenhagen, as he had done in 1883, when he had been entertained by the royal family, but made several vigorous excursions on Norwegian land. Gladstone as a young man had always travelled to Scotland by sea when he could, and chose this cruise as much for refreshment as for his political interest in small nations.[29]

He returned on 3 September to find the party extremists at war. Hartington was proclaiming that no government could concede what Parnell wanted and Chamberlain saying that no Liberal government was worth joining unless committed to compulsory powers enabling local authorities to buy land for social purposes, to free education and to equalization of taxation (the unauthorized programme). The position of the moderates may be put in Derby's words — 'union among Liberals is possible only under Gladstone, and while he lives'.[30] At this juncture, Gladstone issued his Address to the electors of Midlothian. Published in Edinburgh and Manchester on 17 September it sold on the streets of London as a small tract at 1d. It was issued without consulting any colleagues except Granville who read the proofs and made some criticisms which Gladstone accepted. It was an outstandingly able piece of writing, a set of universally acceptable generalities. Carlingford's view, 'It is very skilful and must have great effect in keeping the party together', was echoed by Spencer, Derby and Granville. But, underneath the generalities, Gladstone's mind during the Norwegian journey had moved away from the central board in Dublin to the things which would have to be taken into account if a separate parliament was to be given to Ireland. He had been reading about the making of the union in 1800 and believed there was 'no justification for taking away the national life of Ireland'. Both Derby and Chamberlain visited Hawarden at the beginning of October. Derby believed he had come away with 'What is, in fact, a declaration in favour of Home Rule'. Gladstone believed that he and Chamberlain were 'pretty well agreed'. From the record he sent to Granville it is clear that with Chamberlain he had not broached Home Rule at all but talked about the unauthorized programme. Chamberlain had encouraged the idea that if the Liberals won the election he should form a government on a limited programme of 'local government, land and registration' and hold over the Irish question.[31] This idea melted away during November, and left him face to face with his own readiness to concede a separate parliament while safeguarding Westminster's supremacy. From 24 November to 5 December the general election was fought. The result was indecisive: the Parnellites had given the Irish vote to the Tories but neither party had an overall majority and eighty-six Irish Nationalists had been returned. Salisbury continued in office. Between 7 and 10 December Spencer, Rosebery and Granville came at different times to Hawarden and before or after that visit went to Hartington at Chatsworth where Harcourt was also staying. Here the talk was of Ireland; elsewhere Chamberlain was canvassing the three points of his Radical programme. As late as

15 December there was still no party division between Gladstonians and Unionists. On 17 December the *Standard* followed by the *Pall Mall Gazette* and other papers announced Gladstone's intention to give Ireland a separate parliament. This arose from a supposed indiscretion by his son, Herbert – 'the Hawarden kite'. It is now known that Herbert, a convinced Home Ruler, had been driven by fears that Chamberlain was plotting to oust his father by himself going to the country on the Home Rule cry. He had talked to the press to foil Chamberlain. His fears had been implanted by Wemyss Reid, the editor of the local Liberal paper in Herbert's Leeds constituency. There was no sudden conversion to Home Rule.[32] For Gladstone, 'readiness to concede' was distinct from conceding. Gladstone kept silent and after 17 December only published a statement that Herbert's opinion of his views was purely speculative. The so-called 'kite' probably precipitated Derby, Hartington, Northbrook and perhaps Selborne in their several decisions not to join a Gladstone Home Rule government. Of these Hartington was the most outspoken, having committed himself by a public speech.

The stopgap Tory Government under Salisbury had abandoned coercion in Ireland and had enacted a land purchase bill. The Ashbourne Act of July 1885 allowed the State to advance all the money to a tenant wishing to buy his farm, up to a total commitment of £5 million. The Land Act of 1881 had been satisfactorily amended. The Tramways and Labourers Acts had done something along Chamberlain's line of capital development. But Gladstone's wish that the Tories would take up the Irish Nationalists' demands and settle them was not attained. He was led to hope for it by Carnarvon's activities and by his speech in the Lords on 6 July.[33] Salisbury let Carnarvon have his head. Carnarvon, who had been Colonial Secretary and was now Irish viceroy, did not see an Irish national parliament as a threat to imperial unity. He met Parnell in August, discussing conditions on which a separate parliament for Ireland might be provided and three times brought Home Rule before the Cabinet. On 14 December, after the elections, he presented his full plan and the Cabinet rejected it. The elections were in fact crucial, for Salisbury had drawn from them the conclusion that the English elector did not much care about Ireland. The Tories had gained the Irish vote as Salisbury had intended they should. Having had the Irish vote but not having achieved the majority in England, for which he had hoped, he surrendered to the Tory distrust of Carnarvon and his plans. He reverted to coercion: Gladstone and the Radicals thereupon decided that there was no future in a non-party Irish settlement. They brought down the Tory Government with Jesse Collings's amendment to the Address.

Gladstone formed his third Government and Hartington formed the new Unionist splinter party. Chamberlain joined Gladstone but was no Gladstonian. He might perhaps have worked with Gladstone to the advantage of both the Liberal Party and Ireland, for both men had the intellectual courage to plan and carry a radical solution for Irish self-government. But as is well known, Gladstone had slighted the younger man, 'kept him down' in the Cabinet. When he came to make his Government in January 1886 he refused him the Colonial Office though he offered him the Admiralty. Chamberlain took the Local Government Board at his own wish. Chamberlain hoped to introduce bills on English local authorities.[34] The great barrier between them may have been that, both being Radicals in thought, they were each a different kind of Radical: Chamberlain's radicalism was nearer Bentham's Utilitarianism; Gladstone's had been bred in him by the Greek ideal of polity as Aristotle conceived it, tempered by the Christian ideal as he learnt it from Dante and Butler. Of Chamberlain's views Gladstone wrote, 'His socialism repels me. Some day mischief will come.'[35] Moreover, Chamberlain's presence in a government was apt to alienate older colleagues. His Radicalism was tolerable, but his habit of using the press and other outside agencies as a means of coercing his colleagues – he was suspected of the leakages from Cabinet to newspapers that occurred during Gladstone's second ministry – was not. When Chamberlain was invited to take the chair at the Cobden Club dinner there had been a stampede of Whigs from the Club.[36] Chamberlain's ally, Dilke, was kept out of Gladstone's third Government by court proceedings which followed the divorce case against him, which until he was cleared seemed to prove him a liar and perjurer.

Three new men were now to the fore – Rosebery, who had been Lord Privy Seal for a few months in 1885, at the Foreign Office; Campbell-Bannerman at the War Office; John Morley, Chief Secretary for Ireland. Gladstone himself was Lord Privy Seal as well as Prime Minister. Herschell was Lord Chancellor. Spencer was Lord President, Harcourt Chancellor of the Exchequer, Childers Home Secretary, Kimberley Secretary for India. Ripon went to the Admiralty. Granville, whom the Queen insisted should not go back to the Foreign Office, took the Colonies, Trevelyan the new Scottish Office and A.J. Mundella, an old ally, the Board of Trade. The elections had resulted in 333 seats for the Conservatives, 251 for the Liberals and 86 for Irish Home Rulers, so that Gladstone only had a majority if he kept the Irish vote. On 18 February Parliament met and Gladstone on Ireland continued silent. It was not until 13 March that he outlined to the new Cabinet at its second meeting two Irish bills: one, the Home Rule Bill giving Ireland a separate parliament, the other a Land Purchase Bill. Chamberlain and Trevelyan now offered their resignations, which were not finally accepted until the Cabinet adopted the Irish bills on 26 March. Gladstone had tried in vain to delay resignations until the bills were before Parliament. He introduced the Home Rule Bill on 8 April and the Land Bill on 16 April. His line now was to persuade members to vote for the second reading of the former (began 10 May), that is, to accept the bill in principle and to amend it in committee. The chances of the bill's passing seemed to turn on what amendments would be acceptable. He had summoned a party meeting, and it met on 27 May at the Foreign Office and was addressed by him for an hour. Like all Gladstonian occasions it was a success in that it roused admiration and enthusiasm, but a failure in leaving convictions among possible followers of Chamberlain unchanged. Chamberlain summoned his own meeting on 31 May and rallied fifty-seven dissident Liberals to it. He argued that Gladstone's offer of amendment was not to be trusted. The obstacles to agreement were not insurmountable: the bill discontinued Irish representation at Westminster — this was reversed in the 1893 bill; it reserved subjects for the imperial parliament rather than assigned subjects to the Irish parliament — this too was reversed in 1893; the financial arrangements ought to have been negotiable. The explanation was, as Chamberlain later said, that he wanted to kill the bill.[37]

This he did. When the vote was taken on the second reading a little after 1 a.m. on 8 June 1886 the bill had failed by thirty votes. Thirty-three Liberals had voted in the 343 against the bill. Parliament was dissolved. Gladstone embarked on his election campaign in Scotland, speaking as usual despite the Queen's objections, outside his own constituency. The elections began on 1 July and ended with Gladstonians 191, Liberal Unionists 70, Conservatives 316, Irish 85. Gladstone had turned the election into a plebiscite on Home Rule and it had been lost. Salisbury took office again and began the twenty years of resolute government that he had recommended for Ireland in a famous speech on 15 May. The Irish peasants began the 'Plan of Campaign'. Tenants on an estate combined to offer a rent to the landlord. If their offer was refused they paid it into a fund, used either to support evicted tenants or paid over to the landlord when he accepted the reduced rent. It was a trade-union tactic, difficult to use to alienate the British workman from the Liberal Party. The Liberals did not, indeed, lose the working men's votes at this date. They had lost the election in the counties and not in the cities.

Gladstone's strategy over Home Rule resulted from having two aims. One was to settle Ireland in peace; the other was to keep the party united. To achieve the second he kept silent about his intentions until the very eve of introducing the bill lest he provoke argument within the party and cause men to take entrenched positions. But what was needed to achieve the first was patient persuasion of individuals by the disclosure of his intentions. Moreover, to keep silent for the sake of unity was to put party before conviction, to betray the Gladstonian Liberalism of the sixties. Yet, he claimed, he relied on 'a healthful, slow fermentation in many minds, working towards the final product'.[38] Spencer while wishing for a more open approach yet saw that to disclose his intention to yield to the Nationalists would cause them to raise their demands and try to get more on land purchase. By silence Gladstone lost as much as he gained, for some of the Liberals were provoked to 'open revolt' by his silence.[39] Yet he chose the course that suited him: he was never good at persuasion individual by individual.

From 1886 to 1892 Gladstone was again out of office. The Tories enacted a second land purchase act in 1888 which provided further money to buy out the landlords. It benefited from the report of the Cowper Commission of Enquiry at once set up by Salisbury in 1886. Balfour secured a coercion act of extreme severity without time limit. Ireland was quieter in 1888 than it had been for a generation. Gladstone's attention was partly given to the winning back of the Liberal vote, but he did not take the initiative. This was passing into younger hands. The Round Table Conference that met at Harcourt's house on 14 June 1887 did so with Gladstone's assent but not under his lead. Harcourt's effort to bring back Chamberlain, Trevelyan and others centred on the disputed matters of May 1886 to which Ulster was added, its loyalty to the Union having been made plain by Randolph Churchill. There were two more meetings but the enterprise failed. The initiative was also taken in the constituencies by local Liberal Associations. But they were driving the party in new directions, away from Ireland towards the disestablishment of the Church in Scotland, Wales and England and towards social reform. Gladstonian Liberalism was really over.

There was certainly some return of Liberals to the party and some revival of Liberal activity, so that J.L. Hammond wrote[40] that if Gladstone had come back in 1890 instead of 1892 he might well have carried to the statute-book the Home Rule Bill he introduced in 1893. Hammond thought that the Liberal vote was kept down in the general election of 1892 by the events associated with the fall of Parnell. These began when *The Times* ran a series of articles, 'Parnellism and Crime', which on 18 April 1887 included an alleged letter from Parnell written on 13 May 1882 and seeming to condone the Phoenix Park murders. A further letter appeared during a libel case against *The Times* brought by someone mentioned in the articles. Parnell brought no case, but he eventually asked for an enquiry by the Commons. This it refused but in August 1888 the Government appointed a Commission of three judges before whom was rehearsed the whole history of Irish outrages. When it got to the letters on 14 February 1889, the truth came out. The letters had been forged by one Pigott, who confessed and then killed himself in Madrid. Parnell's counsel, among whom H.H. Asquith distinguished himself, withdrew on the ground that the Commission was not impartial. It finally reported on 13 February 1890, clearing Parnell of all the charges against him. Some, as Gathorne Hardy's *Diary* shows, were not convinced.[41] Others thought Parnell a hero. The Tory majority in the House of Commons received the report, thanked the judges, but made no kind of restitution to Parnell nor to other Irish Nationalists. Gladstone made one of his great orations on Parnell's behalf in the House. As so often happened with single speeches, it drew applause from both sides but changed nothing. He was, meanwhile, working on the details of a new Home Rule Bill and Parnell stayed at Hawarden from 18 to 20 December 'to compare notes'. But Gladstone, though he strove for justice to Parnell, found it difficult to trust him and the effort at co-operation which had come at last came too late.

On 24 December 1889 Captain O'Shea had filed a petition for divorce and court proceedings began in November 1890. O'Shea's motives were connected with disappointed hopes of a share in a fortune inherited by his wife. For her part, Mrs O'Shea accused her husband of collusion and adultery. The rebuttal of these charges occasioned an account of Parnell's life with Mrs O'Shea which made him out a coward, a liar and a perjurer as well as an adulterer. Parnell lost his standing with the Catholics, Irish and English, the Nonconformists and the Radicals. The Irish Nationalist party stood by him and he was indeed re-elected leader. But to Gladstone it seemed that the only hope of winning the next election and bringing in his Home Rule Bill was to get Parnell out of the way. His instrument was a letter to John Morley which Morley read to Parnell and published the same evening. The letter, dated 24 November, included the passage 'If he [i.e., Parnell] does not go, my leadership of the Liberal Party is reduced to a nullity'. Faced with the choice between Parnell and Gladstone, the Irish Nationalists in the Commons split, forty-five declaring against Parnell, twenty-two supporting him. Parnell's career was over and he died at Brighton on 6 October 1891.

These events may have helped to keep the Liberal vote down in 1892, but Liberals of the old Gladstonian variety were unlikely to vote for the programme the party offered at Newcastle in 1891. In October 1891 the National Federation of Liberal Associations had held a conference of delegates at Newcastle. It was the fifth of such party meetings which had begun in a very small way at Nottingham in 1887. A series of resolutions was passed by the Council of the Federation at the Newcastle meeting. They dealt with things that had been crowded out by the pressure on parliamentary time from Gladstone's first Government onwards, but they also included the disestablishment and disendowment of the Church in Wales and Scotland and the three points of Chamberlain's unauthorized programme. Newer Liberals would not be inclined to vote for a party that offered such an incoherent set of aims. This situation was obscured because Gladstone, 'instead of, as was anticipated, devoting his speech at the great Public Meeting [which followed the Council meeting] to the subject of Ireland, took up *seriatim* the resolutions which had been passed at the Council meetings and gave them the weight of his direct approval'.[42] The newspapers at once spoke of the 'Newcastle Programme', and the name stuck.

Gladstone had shown once again, as in the 'snap' dissolution of January 1874, his incapacity to judge how what he did or said would seem to others or to the electorate. He had not intended to produce a programme. He had never thought of liberalism as a dynamo for generating party programmes to win general elections. Gladstonian Liberalism may have stood for free trade; low taxation and low expenditure; a European foreign policy and international justice; institutional reform; individual freedom. In itself, however, it was an attitude of mind, a method, a way of governing the country. The most important part of this to Gladstone was the free share in it of all men. 'For fifty years,' he wrote to Lord Rendel, 'public life in England has been an almost unbroken struggle for emancipation'.[43] Liberalism centred on the idea of enlarging freedom by breaking down privilege and other barriers to the individual's share in the national polity. In his last crusade for the Armenians in 1895 he was to activate this element in Liberalism once again. But he tended for England to think of this struggle for emancipation in the past tense, as if it had been won. Gladstonian Liberalism had really been brought to an end by Chamberlain and his proposals for social reconstruction as well as by Home Rule. 'I look back with pleasure,' he told Rosebery in 1889, 'to the times of liberation in which my political life was cast, and with doubt to the coming times of construction.'[44]

His views on Liberalism explain why it is so difficult to describe Gladstone's attitude to party and its organization. He was neither indifferent to it nor an active participator in it. He watched the parliamentary party with the closest attention. The party whips wrote and spoke to him continually. Glynn (later Wolverton) had sent an analysis of any important division on the following day, apologized for anything that went wrong, sent him his notebook recording the attendance of back-benchers and ministers and the way they voted and made suggestions of what Gladstone might do to raise the spirits of the party or correct anything unfavourable.[45] Gladstone in return helped; he acted when asked but did not interfere with what was the whips' business. He watched by-elections with the minutest scrutiny and he helped by speaking, by small gifts of money, by suggestions of a line to be taken, by reading and replying to the whips' or agents' reports on them. Gladstone's speaking outside his own constituency was well known, and an innovation when it happened after election writs had been issued. In the same way he watched the activities of the registration societies and the local Liberal Associations which replaced them, and helped them when asked. He was present at the inaugural meeting of the National Liberal Federation in 1877 (see p. 80) and later corresponded with successive presidents, Sir James Kitson and Robert Spence Watson, and spoke when asked. There was no direction from him and his speeches were about policy, not about organization. Indeed, both presidents disliked the Birmingham way of organizing this constituency when it had three members (1865) and the tradition which it started.

Gladstone similarly observed sectional politics, corresponding with the Lord Advocate on Scottish questions or several of the Welsh MPs. Stuart Rendel, their leader from 1888, became his closest friend after 1894. But between 1881 and 1894, when Gladstone gained a peerage for him, he constantly visited Gladstone; over Welsh disestablishment, the cause he had most at heart, he constantly took Gladstone's advice. Gladstone took no initiative. Thus Gladstone had three functions in relation to party: he was the great inspirer – one could almost say its *raison d'être*; he was the only integrating element of local, regional, sectional and parliamentary politics, which was not the function of the National Liberal Federation nor claimed by it; he was the fountain-head, the source of advice, help, guidance, whatever was outside the individual power of other agencies. He was not a centralizer like Chamberlain, nor a salesman like Randolph Churchill, nor even an organizer as Cobden had been or later 'city bosses' were. Gladstone's speech at Newcastle is misleading, if it is interpreted as showing that he was himself moving in a new direction. He remained in politics only for the sake of Home Rule. It had become a fixed idea. He no longer applied doctrines of approximation and adaptation. Over Home Rule in and after 1886 he was implacably committed.

The Liberals narrowly won the election of July 1892. When told the final results, a majority of forty for Home Rule, Gladstone, who was staying with Rosebery at Dalmeny, replied 'too small, too small' to someone who remarked that it was sufficient.[46] The Home Rulers, with 355 votes (made up of 273 Liberals, 81 Irish and 1 Labour) to 315 Unionists, were wholly dependent on the Irish members for a majority. Gladstone's own campaign in Midlothian had been a dismal failure. The old enthusiasm had completely evaporated: he secured the seat by a narrow majority, 5,845 to 5,155. Salisbury decided to meet Parliament before resigning which gave the Liberals a month to rally their energies, but there is no sign that Gladstone made any real effort to rally the party. On 7 August the rising young Herbert Asquith was chosen to move the vote of censure and the debate ended with the Tory defeat on the 11th. On 13 August a reluctant Queen sent for Gladstone.

There were no surprises among the members of his fourth Government. Gladstone was again Lord Privy Seal as well as Prime Minister. From all three previous administrations there survived Spencer who took the Admiralty, Kimberley who became Lord President and Secretary for India, and also Ripon who went to the Colonial Office. Harcourt, a survivor from the second administration, was Chancellor of the Exchequer. Rosebery, as Foreign Secretary, just qualified as a survivor, too. Others had only been in the third administration: Herschell as Lord Chancellor, Campbell-Bannerman at the War Office, John Morley as Chief Secretary for Ireland, Trevelyan at the Scottish

Office and A.J. Mundella at the Board of Trade. The new men were: Asquith at the Home Office, James Bryce as Chancellor of the Duchy of Lancaster, G.J. Shaw-Lefèvre, H.H. Fowler (Local Government), A.H.D. Acland (Education), and Arnold Morley (Post Office). Only five of the seventeen sat in the House of Lords, where the Liberals were weaker than ever. There were said to be only twenty-five Liberal peers. A bad sign for the future was a ruling quartet − a Cabinet within the Cabinet − of Gladstone, Rosebery, Harcourt and Morley. Gladstone handled this Cabinet most clumsily. When it met for the first time at 1 Carlton Gardens − it did not move to 10 Downing Street until 1893 − he arranged its members in chairs round the walls of the room and he sat at a small table with Rosebery at his right hand. There was no central table with writing materials.[47] This suited Gladstone's aloofness but did not make for informal discussion or harmony. The Cabinet was dogged from first to last by fierce personal animosities. These centred on Harcourt, witty, egoistical, bludgeoning, and his intriguing son, Lewis ('Loulou'). Morley detested Harcourt and was alternately flattered and used by Loulou. Gladstone's relations with Rosebery steadily deteriorated.

Rosebery had no need of Gladstone. He kept foreign policy in his own hands, failed to consult the Prime Minister, and over Uganda and Egypt and in his general attitude to imperial expansion effectively opposed him. In order to get his way over Uganda, Rosebery was obliged to hoodwink Gladstone if not the rest of the Cabinet. This territory was administered by the chartered British East Africa Company. When Rosebery took office the Company was in such difficulties that it planned to evacuate. In September the Cabinet divided, Rosebery arguing for British annexation, Gladstone with Asquith, Morley, Spencer, Herschell, Ripon and Harcourt against the extension of British responsibilities. Gladstone wrote, 'It is the *first* time, during a Cabinet experience of 22 or 23 years, that I have known the Foreign Minister and the Prime Minister to go before a Cabinet on a present question with diverging views'.[48] Cabinets on 7 and 11 November were again divided on Uganda, and discussion stormy and acrimonious, with Rosebery threatening resignation. Compromise was reached in a decision to send Gerald Portal as Commissioner to enquire. It was, of course, a victory for Rosebery. Portal was most carefully briefed by Rosebery to report in favour of British annexation and there is ground for seeing Rosebery's hand in the final version of his report.[49] The annexation of Uganda followed on 12 April 1894, after Rosebery became Prime Minister.

In the third week of December Gladstone went off to Biarritz. When he returned in January 1893 he was at once faced with a new dispute with Rosebery. This time over Egypt. Cabinets were as stormy as over Uganda. Gladstone harked back to the policy of 1880–82 of agreement with France over Egypt and he was apt to have the support of Kimberley, Spencer and Herschell. Rosebery took the view that British paramountcy depended on the presence of the British garrison and when the British Agent asked for it to be strengthened it must be reinforced. Rosebery had the strong and open support of the Queen and carried his point. Rosebery in Gladstone's opinion was imbued with the spirit of territorial grab.

Apart from these difficulties with Rosebery, Gladstone was wholly taken up with the second Home Rule Bill. He introduced it into the House of Commons on 13 February 1893. It passed its second reading on 21 April by 347 votes to 304 and then went into committee (sixty-three sittings). Gladstone's agility and resource in face of amendments and obstruction 'stirred the wonder and admiration of the House'.[50] It passed its third reading in August. The Commons had given eighty-nine sittings to it in all: on one occasion, violence broke out on the floor of the House. On 9 September 1893 the Lords rejected it on second reading after only four nights' debate by 419 votes to 41. Gladstone was bitterly disappointed not least with Rosebery's witty and pointed but unconvincing speech.

Whatever the course taken by the Government after this setback, it was clear that it was running up a bill against the Lords which sooner or later would have to be paid. They had drastically amended the Government's Employers' Liability Bill and its Parish Councils Bill. Meanwhile, as in 1880–85, the Government's back-bench following and especially the Radicals among them, were being alienated by the ever-growing accumulation of legislative arrears. A dangerous sign of workers' disaffection in the constituencies was the formation of the Independent Labour Party under Keir Hardie. In the autumn there was a national miners' strike. It was Rosebery who brought this to an end with a skilful piece of arbitration on 17 November. It has been said that the reputation of only two Ministers grew during this disastrous year, those of Asquith for his management of domestic legislation in the Commons and of Rosebery for his conduct of foreign policy.

The final break-up was brought about by a dispute on naval policy. The Board of Admiralty had presented Spencer with a 'desirable' programme of building and a 'minimum' one. In December, foreseeing the impossibility of passing anything else, he chose the minimum. Anything less would have brought the resignation of the whole Board of Admiralty. Harcourt as Chancellor of the Exchequer battled against estimates for naval building according to this programme, subjecting Spencer to a deluge of fierce memoranda throughout December. If Spencer thought of retiring to buy horses, he was quite ready to go to Malwood and grow cabbages. Rosebery, on the other hand, thought the estimates were too low and worked for an increase of the navy. When Harcourt gave way, Gladstone, who thought he only did so for fear he might lose the chance of presenting a budget with reformed and graduated death duties, was isolated in his own Cabinet. There was then (19 December) a debate in the Commons on Lord George Hamilton's motion calling for 'a considerable addition to the navy' and for a statement from the Prime Minister on naval policy. Gladstone spoke but so ambiguously as to satisfy neither Rosebery nor Spencer. He was pursuing the old policy of being obscure so as to keep his Cabinet together. It was decided to postpone a final decision until early in the New Year.

The crucial Cabinet met on 9 January 1894. It was as remote as possible from an informal discussion. Rosebery describes how Gladstone addressed it for fifty minutes and congratulated himself on ending within the hour. Spencer spoke for five or six conciliatory minutes. Harcourt then launched into a ferocious counterpart to Gladstone's address. It was agreed to frame estimates according to Spencer's programme. Gladstone announced that he proposed to leave for Biarritz on Saturday, 13 January. This he did, but before he went, Morley, deputed by his colleagues, had broken it to Mrs Gladstone that the long reign was over. It was only a question whether Gladstone should finally retire then or wait until he returned in February. From Biarritz, Gladstone sent messages which showed that he thought of dissolving and going to the country on the issue of Lords versus people. When he returned to Downing Street in February 1894 suspense about his retirement was preserved. His first Cabinet after his return on 12 February discussed the Lords' amendments to the two bills just mentioned. The Cabinet dinner on 17 February passed without any indication. On 23 February the Cabinet discussed the Queen's Speech to end the 1893–94 session. At the close of the next Cabinet on 1 March Gladstone spoke in general terms of his co-operation with the Cabinet being at an end, he should retire on grounds of health. There were some quiet remarks of farewell and regret to which Gladstone was beginning to reply when Harcourt took out of his pocket both a large handkerchief and a manuscript and embarked on a eulogy. Gladstone, who called it afterwards the 'blubbering' Cabinet, listened with 'hooded eyes and

tightened lips'.[51] The Queen sent for Rosebery. She had not asked
Gladstone (who would have recommended Lord Spencer) for his
advice. The busy activity of 'Loulou' Harcourt, William Harcourt and
John Morley during the last eighteen months of struggle for the
succession evaporated as if it had never been. Gladstone did not stand
in the general election of 1895.

Gladstone's political career was over. He had never been a politician
and always disclaimed that description. He was 'a man in politics'. The
man's life went on, despite deafness and failing sight with cataract in
both eyes. He translated Horace, he worked on the Olympic system of
Gods; he contributed two theological articles to the *Nineteenth Century*
in 1894. In 1895 he published the concordance of the psalms on which
he had been busy intermittently since the fifties; he intervened in the
Sabbatarian controversy in the *Church Monthly* and wrote on Butler in
the *Nineteenth Century*. In 1896 he published his edition of Butler's
Analogy and reviewed Francis Rae's *Sheridan*, 'patriot, orator, statesman' in the *Nineteenth Century*. In January 1898 he wrote 'Personal
Recollections of Arthur H. Hallam' for the *Daily Telegraph*. This was
his last article.

But 'his flame did not yet lack oil'. It flared up when in November
1894 the newspapers became full of Turkish massacres of Armenians.
This was a situation outside one train of Gladstonian thought. Since the
Armenians were scattered throughout Turkish Asia Minor, though
concentrated among Kurds and Circassians round Erzerum and in
Cilicia, nationalism did not apply. There was no question of a national
Armenian state unless the Turkish Empire disappeared altogether. It
was to Gladstone's broad humanity that the Armenians appealed when
a delegation from the Armenian community in England came to
Hawarden on 29 December 1894. He was roused to tell them that the
Turkish Empire should be wiped off the map. But during 1895 Russia,
France and Britain (acting on the Cyprus Convention, see p. 83)
intervened; their consuls enquired and Turkey was presented with a
programme of reforms. Gladstone remained quiet until it was clear how
ineffectual both this intervention and Turkish measures to restore order
were. Then in August 1895 he addressed a great public meeting called
to protest, in Chester. Turkey seemed better able to enforce law and
order during the winter but a fresh bout of killing came in 1896 and
further protest meetings were convened by active sympathisers in
Britain. Gladstone published an article on the massacres in the October
number of the *Nineteenth Century*. It was fitting that his last great

oration — he spoke for an hour and twenty minutes — should have been to the protest meeting at Liverpool (24 September 1896). He did one more thing in 1896. He made arrangements for his large and varied library to become the nucleus of a great library freely open to all at St Deiniol's, Hawarden where those who use it can still stay in a college atmosphere at an attached hostel.

The winters of all these last years were spent in the south of France, mostly at Biarritz or Cannes. At Cannes he stayed in Lord Rendel's house and he and Mrs Gladstone were carefully cosseted by this last close friend. One regular entry in his diary (which he stopped keeping after his birthday of 1896) has so far not been mentioned. This was his daily church attendance. Illness alone caused it to be interrupted. As long as he could walk he kept it up, and after that Catherine was his 'chaplain'. Cancer had set in in 1897 though it was not at once diagnosed. He returned to Hawarden after the winter at Cannes and then went to Bournemouth on 22 March 1898, and died there on Ascension Day. He was brought to Westminster Hall and lay there on 26 and 27 May. There had been one assembly of people at Hawarden, 'black masses of people, thousands and thousands, from Manchester and Liverpool and other manufacturing towns'. Now at Westminster people of all classes and kinds processed past the coffin and tributes were paid from all the nations of Europe, from America and from the Empire. He was buried in Westminster Abbey on 28 May. As Mrs Gladstone entered the Abbey 'the vast concourse of people, seated tier above tier on each side of the nave, spontaneously rose as she walked slowly up the centre'.[52] The pall bearers to the grave included the future George V, Salisbury, Rosebery, Balfour, Spencer, Kimberley, Harcourt and Rendel.

What of the verdict? Hostile criticism can be answered. Gladstone did not wish to increase the Empire, but he did formulate broad principles which allowed the Empire to be preserved in the nineteenth century and to be transformed gradually into the Commonwealth as the Statute of Westminster recorded it in 1931. He was weak in foreign policy, but he did formulate standards of international co-operation and just action. He abandoned Gordon, but the Egyptian peasant owed a debt of gratitude to British administration and the prosperity of Egypt and, later, of the Sudan was based on the opportunities he had opened up by his policy. He was too 'European', but he improved relations with the United States and had American correspondents and never lost interest in federal constitutions. He destroyed the Irish Church, but that was the logical conclusion of the evolution of the pluralist state to which he had accommodated his ecclesiastical ideas ever since 1845. The Irish Church which replaced the English Church in Ireland was a viable institution owing to the provisions of a good act. He would have separated Ireland from the rest of Britain, but had he succeeded in 1886 or 1893 he would have done it without civil war, though no one can tell whether war might not have happened afterwards, unless of course Ulster had been able to make terms with a Dublin parliament. His reforms disturbed the social equilibrium, but the financial administration of the fifties and sixties, like the free-trade policy of the forties, had encouraged the harmony of classes and was keyed into the broad lines of economic development and was a support for social peace. He was a demagogue, exciting his massed audiences to political action, but he was also a great political educator and the principal architect of political democracy as it was shaped by the parliamentary reforms of 1866–68 and 1884–85. Chamberlain in 1885–86 destroyed Gladstonian Liberalism by his unauthorized programme but it had earlier produced a great ministry in 1868–74. Salisbury, perhaps Gladstone's nearest equal in both statesmanship and churchmanship, however different their opinions, spoke of him in the House of Lords, asking the cause of the unaminity of feeling when Gladstone died:

> Of course, he had qualities which distinguished him from other men; and you may say that it was this transcendent intellect, his astonishing power of attaching men to him, and the great influence he was able to exert upon the thought and convictions of his contemporaries. . . It was [rather] on account of considerations more common to the masses of human beings, to the general working of the human mind. . . He will leave behind him the memory of a great Christian statesman. . .[53]

Notes

Notes to Chapter 1

[1]S.G. Checkland, *The Gladstones, A Family Biography, 1764–1851* (Cambridge, 1971) supplies most of the information about the family used in this chapter.

[2]All notices of Gladstone's reading, movements and much else are taken from his diary, references to which are in the form: *Diaries*, i. 9 Apr. 27; *The Gladstone Diaries* (Oxford, 1968–):

volume 1, 1825–32, edited M.R.D. Foot (1968)
volume 2, 1833–39, edited M.R.D. Foot (1968)
volume 3, 1840–47, edited M.R.D. Foot and H.C.G. Matthew (1974)
volume 4, 1848–54, edited M.R.D. Foot and H.C.G. Matthew (1974)
volume 5, 1855–60, edited H.C.G. Matthew (1978)
volume 6, 1861–68, edited H.C.G. Matthew (1978)
volume 7, 1869–71, edited H.C.G. Matthew (1982)
volume 8, 1871–74, edited H.C.G. Matthew (1982)
volume 9, 1875–80, edited H.C.G. Matthew (1986)
volume 10, 1881–

[3]*Diaries*, i. 5 Aug. 28.

[4]*Diaries*, i. 19, 20, 22, 26 Nov. 28; John Morley, *The Life of William Ewart Gladstone* (London, 1903), vol. 1, pp. 635–41.

[5]Morley, 1, p. 82; cp., *Diaries*, i. 17 Jan. 32.

[6]Banker is only mentioned when he gets lost, at Pozzuoli, *Diaries*, i. 18 May 32, and on the way to Karlsruhe, 20 Jul. 32.

[7]*Diaries*, i. 10 Mar. 32.

[8]*Diaries*, for the first effect 2 Feb. 32; for the last effect 13 May 32 at Naples. See also Perry Butler, *Gladstone: Church, State and Tractarianism* (Oxford, 1982), pp. 21–37; and Boyd Hilton, 'Gladstone's Theological Politics' in M. Bentley and J. Stevenson, *High and Low Politics in Modern Britain* (Oxford, 1983), pp. 28–57.

[9]*Diaries*, i. 6 Jul. 32.

[10]See *Parliamentary Papers*, Reports of Committees in each of the years 1835–40.

[11]'On books and the housing of them', *Nineteenth Century*, xxvii, p. 384 (Mar. 1890); *Diaries*, iii. 18, 25 Jul. 40; 3, 11, 20, 27 Feb., 5 Mar., 26 Apr. 41.

[12]*Diaries*, iii. 25 Aug. 41.

[13]Blaise Pascal, *Pensées* ed. Pleiade, trans. M. Turnell (1962), p. 165.

[14]See the essay 'The rule of faith', British Library, Add. MS 44726, fos. 155–74.

[15]*Diaries*, ii. 20, 27 Aug. 37 (Sundays). The references to Coleridge are strengthened in the 1841 edition of *The State in its Relations with the Church*.

[16]'Gladstone on Church and State' in *Edinburgh Review* (April 1839); reprinted in *Critical and Historical Essays* (Everyman edition, 1907), vol. 2, pp. 237–89.

[17]*The State in its Relations with the Church* (fourth edition, 1841), vol. 2, p. 262.

[18]*Diaries*, i. 3–8, 11, 12, 26 Oct., 1 Nov. 31.

[19]See in addition to the *Diaries*, A. Tilney Bassett (ed.), *Gladstone to his Wife* (1936); Mary Drew, *Catherine Gladstone* (1919); G. Battiscombe, *Mrs Gladstone* (1956).

[20]*Diaries*, iii. 16 Apr., 42 and Bassett, p. 42.

[21]J. Prest, *Lord John Russell* (1972), p. 173; F.E. Hyde, *Mr Gladstone at the Board of Trade* (1934), p. 213. N. Gash, *Sir Robert Peel. Life after 1850* (1972), chapter 9 deals with the changes of 1842 from Peel's side.

[22]Hyde, p. 43, footnote sets out both scales. Hyde's account of the arguments with Peel needs revision in the light of the *Diaries*.

[23]J. Brooke and M. Sorensen, *The Prime Minister's Papers: W.E. Gladstone* (1971–2), vol. 1, p. 127, mem. on recorded errors, 7 Nov. 1896, vol. 2, pp. 169–72.

[24]R. Blake, *Disraeli* (1966), pp. 329–30.

[25]P. Butler, *Gladstone: Church, State and Tractarianism* (1982), pp. 111–31.

[26]*Diaries*, iii. end of mem. attached to entry of 4 Mar. 44.

[27]The information about these three articles is from Gladstone's correspondence with Worthington, Add. MS 44359, fos. 238, 291; 44360, fos. 118, 133, 239, 243, 245, 249; 44527, fo. 106.

[28]*Diaries*, iii. 22 Dec. 45, 5 Aug. 47, note 6.

[29]Gladstone to Cathcart, no. 14, 3 Feb. 1846, copy in Public Record Office 30/29/57; see A. Ramm (ed.) *The Political Correspondence of Mr Gladstone and Lord Granville 1868–76* (1952) vol. 1, pp. 24, 89, 91; Add. MS 44738, fos. 234–63. I am indebted throughout to Susan Farnsworth, *The Evolution of British Imperial Policy during the mid-nineteenth Century: the Peelite Contribution 1846–74*, unpublished PhD thesis, Brandeis University 1983, but see especially pp. 57–66; cp. Morley, vol. 1, p. 358–64.

[30]Farnsworth, p. 62.

[31]Gladstone to Cathcart, 3 Feb. 46, quoted by Farnsworth, p. 17.

[32]Add. MS 44738, fo. 245, quoted by Farnsworth, p. 59.

[33]*Diaries*, iii. 13 Jun. 40.

[34]*Diaries*, iii. 23 Feb. 45 and note.

[35]See Philip Magnus, *Gladstone. A Biography* (1954), pp. 81–7.

[36]*Diaries*, iv. 21 Feb. 48; cp. 8, 19 Aug. 48.

[37]Ibid., 2 Jul. 50.

[38]The last four paragraphs follow diary entries closely.

Notes to Chapter 2

[1]*Diaries*, iv. 14 May 51. It was a meeting of coal-whippers who unloaded cargoes of coal in the port of London. He had been concerned in two bills protecting their interests, in 1843 and 1851, *Diaries*, iv. 6 Jun. 51 and note; *Parliamentary Papers* (1851) vol. 2, bills 206 and 524.

[2]E. Drus (ed.), *A Journal of Events during the Gladstone Ministry, 1868–74, by John First Earl of Kimberly* (Royal Historical Society, Camden Series, 1958), p. 22, 29 Apr. 1871.

[3]Everything about Leopardi touched Gladstone's imagination from the time when he read the vivid account of the poet's last days (1837) in Vicenzo Gioberti, *Il Gesuita moderno*, *Diaries*, iv. 4 May–18 Jun., 24 Aug.–11 Sept., 16 Sept.–12 Dec. 48. When immersed in Homer he became interested in the poet's philological learning and critical powers. In July 1849 in Rome he bought the four volume edition of the *Opere* and began to read the *Canti*, *Diaries*, iv. 28 Jul. 49. The March 1850 number of the *Quarterly* contained Gladstone's much noticed review of the *Opere*. He ranges Leopardi with Dante, Milton, Cowper, Shelley and Coleridge. See also D.E. Rhodes, 'The Composition of Mr Gladstone's Essay on Leopardi', *Italian Studies* viii, p. 70 (1953).

[4]The composition and publication of the two *Letters to Aberdeen* may be followed in *Diaries*, iv. at the appropriate dates.

[5]*Diaries*, iv. 12 Nov. 51. It is significant that he sent this to the Whiggish *Edinburgh Review*, not to the *Quarterly*. See number for Apr. 1852 and Gladstone to Lacaita, 11 Oct. 1855, Add. MS 44233, fo. 66, The *Quarterly*, xc, p. 226 (Dec. 1851) had a hostile review of his translation.

[6]See H.L. Cole, *Fifty Years of Public Work of Sir Henry Cole* (2 vols., 1884); *Parliamentary Papers* (1852), xxvi, p. 1, 'First Report of the Commissioners of 1851'; ibid. (1852–53), liv, p. 407 for second report.

[7]*Diaries*, iv. 16, 17 Dec. 52; *Hansard*, cxxiii, 1523, 1666; Blake, *Disraeli*, pp. 328–47.

[8]H.C.G. Matthew, 'Disraeli, Gladstone and the Politics of Mid-Victorian Budgets', *Historical Journal*, xxii, pp. 620–9 (Oct. 1979).

[9]See Olive Anderson, *A Liberal State at War* (1967), pp. 13, 194–216.

[10]In the sense of fervour for Ottoman loyalty.

[11]This account draws on A. Ramm in *New Cambridge Modern History*, (Cambridge, 1960), vol. 10, pp. 468 ff.

[12]G. Cornewall Lewis to Graham, 23 Aug. 1853, C.S. Parker, *Life and Letters of Sir James Graham* (2 vols., London, 1907) vol. 2, p. 206; Blake, *Disraeli*, p. 356; Morley, vol. 1, p. 508.

[13]*Diaries*, iv. 9 May 54.

[14]*Gladstone to his Wife*, pp. 105–6.

[15]Brooke and Sorenson, *The Prime Minister's Papers*, vol. 1, pp. 131–2, mem. on recorded errors, 7 Nov. 96.

[16]*Diaries*, v. 16 Feb. 56.

[17]Ibid., v. 1 Apr. 56.

[18]Ibid., v. 17 Apr. 56 and attached memorandum.

[19]Ibid., v. 16 Apr. 56.

[20] *Hansard*, cxlii. 96, 6 May 1856.

[21] Ibid., cxlii. 98, 6 May 1856.

[22] *Diaries*, v. 20 Dec. 56 and note 5.

[23] *Diaries*, v. 20, 23 Jan., 3, 4 Feb. with attached record of conversation with Derby, 5, 10, 11 Feb. and attached record of conversation with Derby, 14 Feb. and attached mem. 16, 19, 20 Feb. 57 and note 7.

[24] *Diaries*, v. 3 Mar. 57, 'voted in 263:247 − a division doing more honour to the H of C than any I ever remember'; Morley, vol. I, p. 563 quoting Phillimore, a close friend of Gladstone.

[25] Gladstone to Elwin, declining invitation to review Guizot's *Peel*, 27 Mar. 57, *Diaries*, v. p. 207 note 4.

[26] *Diaries*, v. 31 Mar. 57 with attached letter to Aberdeen; cp. Parker, *Graham*, vol. 2, p. 309.

[27] *Diaries*, v. 14 Feb. 57.

[28] Ibid., p. 19, mem. following entry 5 Feb. 55.

[29] Ibid., v. p. 358, mem. following entry 28 Dec. 58.

[30] *Diaries*, iii. 6 Nov. 46.

[31] W.E. Gladstone, *Studies on Homer and the Homeric Age* (3 vols., Oxford, 1858), vol. 1, p. 361.

[32] *Studies*, vol. 3, p. 2–3.

[33] Ibid., p. 7.

[34] Ibid., pp. 122–3.

[35] Ibid., p. 392.

[36] *Diaries*, v. 24 Aug. 58; for Ariosto with Willie and Agnes, 17, 19 Aug. 58; for woodcutting see, e.g. 31 Jul. 58, 2 Aug. 58.

[37] *Diaries*, v. 5 Nov. 60 and note.

[38] *Diaries*, vi. 10 Oct. 61.

[39] Ibid., 23 Apr. 62.

[40] Ibid., 7–9, 22 Oct. 62; 27 Dec. 62; 26 Oct. 63 published as 'Wedgwood: an Address' (1863), reprinted in W.E. Gladstone, *Gleanings of Past Years* (1879), vol. 2, p. 181; 11, 14 Oct. 64.

[41] See F.B. Smith, *The Making of the Second Reform Bill* (1966), p. 10 for the first quotation; *Diaries*, v. pp. xxxii, xliv–xlvi; cp. J. Vincent, *The Formation of the British Liberal Party* (2nd edition 1976), pp. 58–65, who refers to Gladstone's astute use of the press

[42] T. Bassett (ed.), *Gladstone to his Wife* (1936), p. 126, 17 Sept. 59.

[43] *Diaries*, v. 7 Jul., 13 Sept. 59 and notes.

[44] Cp. Drus, p. 22.

[45] *Diaries*, v. 18 Jul. 59 and note 15; 30 Nov. 59; 'Cabinet 3–6, I found myself very *lonely* on the question of Military Estimates'.

[46] See A. Ramm (ed.), *The Political Correspondence of Mr Gladstone and Lord Granville 1876–86* (1962), vol. 1, no. 194.

[47] *Diaries*, v. 31 Jan. 60; see also J. Morley, *The Life of Richard Cobden* (one vol. edition, 1903), pp. 702–30; *Diaries*, v. 12, 13 Sept. 59; 11, 13, 15, 23 Jan. 60; 10 Feb. 60 and note.

[48] See, for all Gladstone's work as Chancellor of the Exchequer, H.C.G. Matthew, 'Disraeli, Gladstone and the Politics of Mid-Victorian Budgets', *Historical Journal*, xxii, pp. 615–43 (Oct. 1979) and his introduction to *Diaries*, v. pp. xxix–xxxvii.

[49]Morley, vol. 1, p. 628.

[50]D. Beales, *England and Italy 1859–60* (1961), pp. 90–1.

[51]Ibid., p. 103.

[52]*Diaries*, v. memorandum following entry of 30 Jun. 59.

[53]Ibid., 28 Oct. 59 and para. 5 of mem. following entry of 7 Jan. 60.

[54]Beales, pp. 118–19.

[55]*Diaries*, v. 2 Jun. 60.

[56]*Diaries*, vi. 19 Mar. 62, memorandum at pp. 103–8.

[57]Ibid., 25 Jul. 65.

[58]*Diaries*, iv. 23 Nov. 53.

[59]Graham to Lord John Russell, 27 Nov. 1858, Parker, *Graham*, vol. 2, pp. 359–60. See also *Diaries*, v. 3, 4 Sept. 58.

[60]*Diaries*, v. 29 Mar. 59 and note 11.

[61]Ibid., vi. 11 May 64 and note 4.

[62]Ibid., 8, 10, 12 Mar. 66.

[63]Ibid., 5 Apr. 66.

[64]Ibid., 27 Apr. and note 1, 28 Apr. 66; F.B. Smith, *The Making of the Second Reform Bill*, p. 90–1.

[65]Smith, p. 103 quoting Gladstone to Russell, 28 May; *Diaries*, vi. 31 May 66.

[66]*Diaries*, vi. 19 Jun. 66; cp. Smith, p. 115 quoting Gladstone to Russell, 20 Jun. 66.

[67]Smith, pp. 167, 174 quoting an undated mem. by Gladstone.

[68]*Diaries*, vi. 12 Apr. 67.

[69]Ibid., 11 Jul. 67 and note 16.

[70]See *Quarterly Review*, cxxiv, p. 199 (Jan. 1868).

[71]W.E. Gladstone, *Juventus Mundi, The Gods and Men of the Heroic Age* (London, 1869), p. 38.

[72]Ibid., p. 174.

[73]Ibid., p. 179.

[74]Ibid., p. 412.

[75]*Diaries*, v. 31 Dec. 56.

[76]Ibid., 22 Aug. 58.

Notes to Chapter 3

[1]*Diaries*, v. 31 Mar. 57; he told his Oxford constituents in 1865 that the Irish Church establishment was 'indefensible'; 19 Dec. 67 at Southport. The famous 'Upas Tree' speech was at Wigan, 23 October 1868. See also J.P. Parry, *Democracy and Religion* (1986), pp. 176, 266.

[2]*Diaries*, vi. 28 Feb., 10, 13 Jul., 5 Dec. 68.

[3]P. Gordon (ed.), *The Red Earl. The Papers of the Fifth Earl Spencer* (1981, 1986), vol. 1, pp. 6, 72. Drus, pp. 1–2.

[4]Drus, p. 25.

[5]Ibid., p. 2; *Diaries*, vii. 23 Mar. 69; *Gladstone, Granville 1868–76*, (Camden Series, 1952), vol. 1, pp.36, 40–2.

[6]E.D. Steele, *Irish Land and British Politics: tenant-right and nationality* (1974), p. 8. The whole paragraph is based on Steele's book.

[7]Steele, pp. 200–12.

[8]*Gladstone, Granville 1868–76*, vol. 1, pp. 22–3; see also G.M. Trevelyan, *The Life of John Bright* (1925), pp. 349–50.

[9]*Gladstone, Granville 1868–76*, vol. 1, p. 5 and note.

[10]*The Red Earl*, vol. 1, pp. 85, 93–5.

[11]The Irish Republican Brotherhood had been founded in 1858 and superseded the secret ribbon lodges as a main channel of Irish protest, transforming it from a local to a national group. K.T. Hoppen, *Elections, Politics and Society in Ireland* (1984), p. 464.

[12]*Red Earl*, vol. 1, pp. 77–83, 89–90, 108 and notes; *Gladstone, Granville 1868–76*, vol. 1, pp. 90, 92–3, 95 note.

[13]Drus, p. 20.

[14]See *Gladstone, Granville 1868–76*, vol. 1, introduction, p. xiv; *Gladstone, Granville 1876–86* (Oxford, 1962) vol. 1, introduction, pp. xxxvii–xxxix.

[15]*Diaries*, viii. 12 Mar. 73.

[16]A. Ramm, 'The Parliamentary Context of Cabinet Government, 1868–74', *English Historical Review*, xcix (Oct. 1984), p. 759.

[17]*Diaries*, vii. p. lxx, 13 Oct. 70, 6 Mar. 71.

[18]Add. MS 44087, fo. 10.

[19]Drus, p. 30.

[20]*Gladstone, Granville 1868–76*, vol. 2, p. 451.

[21]*Gladstone, Granville 1868–76*, vol. 1, p. 143.

[22]*Diaries*, vi. 22 Oct. 66.

[23]*Diaries*, vii. p. xli.

[24]*Gladstone, Granville 1868–76*, vol. 1, p. 117 for the quotation; see p. 116 note 3 for reference to Foreign Office correspondence on which the Benedetti treaty incident is based.

[25]Granville to Lyons, private 13 Jul. 70, Lord Newton, *Lord Lyons* (1913), p. 298; *Gladstone, Granville 1868–76*, vol. 1, pp. 113, 119 and note 1.

[26]Ibid., pp. 125–31, 133, 135, 146–7, 154, 173, 181 and notes; *Diaries*, vii. memoranda attached to entries 25, 30 Sept., 1, 8 Oct., 7, 23 Nov. 70.

[27]Granville to Buchanan, no. 301, 10 Nov. 70, FO 65/799 follows text of Gladstone's memorandum, *Gladstone, Granville 1868–76*, vol. 1, pp. 154–6; cp. ibid. pp. 161, 168–9.

[28]Granville to Lyons, no. 29 commercial, 27 Jan. 72, FO 27/1934 based on memorandum by Gladstone in *Gladstone, Granville 1868–76*, vol. 2, p. 302, note 6.

[29]Ibid., vol. 2, p. 313 note 2; cp. *Diaries*, vii. 22 Mar. 69 attached letter.

[30]*Gladstone, Granville 1868–76*, vol. 1, p. 209. The whole negotiation may be followed in Gladstone-Granville letters and the notes attached to them.

[31]*Diaries*, vii. 31 Mar., 11 Apr., 71.

[32]For the failure of bills generally see Ramm, 'The Parliamentary Context of Cabinet Government', *English Historical Review*, xcix (Oct. 1984), pp. 754 ff.; see also Drus, pp. 10–11 and note 2, 40.

[33]*Diaries*, viii. 18, 19, 20, 23 Jan. 74 and attached memoranda.

[34]*Diaries*, v. p. lxi. and vii. pp. ciii–cviii and viii appendix.

[35]Granville to Gladstone, 25 June 74, *Gladstone, Granville 1868–76*, vol. 2, p. 455.

[36]Ibid., pp. 456–7 and notes for Harcourt incident, pp. 449–50, 463 for other quotations.

[37] *Diaries*, iii. 10 Jul. 46 attached memorandum. Ibid. ix, pp. 501 and 504 for Granville being the leader with Hartington in second place.

[38] *Gladstone, Granville 1868–76*, vol. 2, p. 487 for conversation with Stratford de Redcliffe; *Diaries*, ix. 27 June, 11, 24, 25, 27, 28, 31 July 76.

[39] *Gladstone, Granville 1868–76*, vol. 2, p. 489.

[40] *Gladstone, Granville 1876–86*, vol. 1, pp. 3, 5.

[41] R. Shannon, *Gladstone and the Bulgarian Agitation* (second edition, 1975) pp. 73, 109, 111, chapter 2 *passim*. *Diaries*, ix. 18, 19 Nov. 75 for J.L. Farley.

[42] The tours, visits and parliamentary attendances can be followed in the *Diaries*; quotations from *Gladstone, Granville 1876–86*, vol. 1, p. 70, and *Diaries*, ix. 7 May 77.

[43] Lord Crewe, *Lord Rosebery* (1931), vol. 1, p. 125; R.R. James, *Rosebery* (1963), pp. 91–7.

[44] *Gladstone, Granville 1876–86*, vol. 1, p. 91.

[45] M.R.D. Foot (ed.), *Midlothian Speeches 1879* (reprint 1971), pp. 42, 101. Cp. *Diaries*, ix. introduction, pp. liv–lxi.

[46] *Diaries*, ix. 30 Mar. 75.

[47] Ibid., 24 June 75.

[48] Ibid., ix. 14 Nov. 78.

[49] Ibid., v. 13 Aug. 59.

[50] *Quarterly Review* (July 1876), reprinted W.E. Gladstone, *Gleanings of Past Years 1843–78* (1879), vol. 2, p. 265. His historical reading may be followed in the *Diaries* from vol. iii onwards.

[51] 'Germany, France and England'; *Edinburgh Review*, vol. cxxxii (Oct. 1870), pp. 555, 561, 578, 593.

[52] *Good Words*, edited by Norman Macleod, vol. ix (Jan, Feb, Mar 1868), pp. 33–9, 80–88, 177–85.

[53] See T.A. Jenkins, 'Gladstone, the Whigs and the leadership of the Liberal party', *Historical Journal* xxvii (1984) pp. 337, 355; *Diaries*, ix. 8 Apr. 80 and note 8, 10–13, 22, 23 Apr. 80 and attached memoranda; see ibid., p. 504 for the Queen's being 'wrong' in not sending for Granville, '*the* leader'.

[54] *Gladstone, Granville1876–86*, vol. 1, p. 43.

[55] *Diaries*, ix. 25 Oct. 80 attached letter to Forster; *Red Earl*, vol. 1, p. 165.

[56] *The Times*, 6 Apr. 80, p. 5e–f and *Gladstone, Granville 1876–86*, vol. 1, p. 118.

[57] Ibid., pp. 178, 181, 19 and 23 Sept. 80.

[58] From Goschen, tel. no. 297, 9 Oct., tel. no. 303, 11 Oct., received 12 Oct. 80, FO. 78/3106; *Pall Mall Gazette*, late edition, 7 Oct. 80; Gladstone to Granville, 13 Oct. 80, *Gladstone, Granville 1876–86*, vol. 1, p. 198.

[59] Ibid., p. 253, 7 Apr. 81.

[60] Ibid., pp. 127 and note 4, 133–4, 216 and note 1.

[61] *Diaries*, iii. 4 Feb. 44.

Notes to Chapter 4

[1]*Diaries*, ix. 17 Oct–11 Nov. 77; K.T. Hoppen, *Elections, Politics and Society in Ireland*, p. 271, refers to the 'energetic myopia' of this tour; *Gladstone, Granville 1876–86*, vol. 1, p. 58; M.R.D. Foot (ed.), *Midlothian Speeches, 1879* (reprint, 1971) p. 88, 26 Nov. 79 at Dalkeith.

[2]*Diaries*, ix. 23 Oct., 17 Nov. 80.

[3]*Diaries*, ix. 29–31 Dec. 80.

[4]Speech at the Guildhall, 6 Aug. 81, *The Times*, 7 Aug. 81.

[5]J.L. Hammond, *Gladstone and the Irish Nation* (second edition, 1964) p. 244.

[6]*Gladstone, Granville 1876–86*, vol. 1, p. 289 note, 296, 298, 299. See also *Red Earl*, pp. 164, 179, 184–9.

[7]*Gladstone, Granville 1876–86*, vol. 1, p. 302, note 1; pp. 291, 293.

[8]*Red Earl*, vol. 1, pp. 207, 225, 229.

[9]Hammond, p. 277.

[10]*Gladstone, Granville 1876–86*, vol. 1, p. 373 note 1. Hammond p. 297.

[11]See A. Ramm, 'Great Britain and France in Egypt', in P. Gifford and W.R. Louis, *France and Britain in Africa* (Yale University Press, 1971), pp. 73–120.

[12]Ramm, 'Egypt', p. 85. Ring to Waddington, no. 1 confidential, 27 Dec. 1879, Ministère d'affaires étrangères, C. P. Egypte 64.

[13]*Gladstone, Granville 1876–86*, vol. 1, pp. 413, 434.

[14]Ibid., p. 331.

[15]Ibid., vol. 2, p. 307; see also A. Ramm, 'Granville' in K.M. Wilson (ed.), *British Foreign Secretaries and Foreign Policy* (1987), pp. 97–8.

[16]*Gladstone, Granville 1876–86*, vol. 2, pp. 369–72, 375–84, 385.

[17]*Red Earl*, vol. 1, p. 224 note 1 to no. 286; *Gladstone, Granville 1876–86*, vol. 1, pp. 450, 451.

[18]See Public Record Office, Granville Papers, 30/29/27A for Hartington; for Irish paragraphs see *Red Earl*, p. 226.

[19]*Gladstone, Granville 1876–86*, vol. 2, pp. 14–15.

[20]*The Times*, 20 Jan. 1883, p. 6c.

[21]*Gladstone, Granville 1876–86*, vol. 2, p. 51; Rathbone to Gladstone, 9 May 83, Add. MS 44480, fo. 309.

[22]Ibid.,, vol. 2, pp. 209–12 and notes.

[23]Add. MSS 44480–96 *passim*.

[24]*Gladstone, Granville 1876–86*, vol. 2, pp. 116, 149–51 and notes.

[25]Ibid., p. 157 note 5, p. 162 note 2, pp. 163, 165, 166, 168, 173, 217.

[26]See Gladstone's Cabinet notes, Add. MS 44645 at appropriate dates.

[27]J.R. Vincent (ed.), *The Later Derby Diaries* (1981) 19, 25 Jul. 85, p. 0027; cp. *Red Earl*, Spencer to Gladstone and reply, 26, 29 Jan. 85, pp. 289–94; pp. 300–5.

[28]*Gladstone, Granville 1876–86*, vol. 2, p. 390.

[29]Morley, vol. 3, pp. 115–17, 215–18.

[30]*Derby Diaries*, 24 Sept. 85, p. 0030.

[31]Ibid., 1 Oct. 85, pp. 0032–3; *Gladstone, Granville 1876–86*, vol. 2, p. 403.

[32]*Red Earl*, vol. 2, pp. 82–3, 86–7; *Derby Diaries*, p. 0047; D.A. Hamer, *Liberal Politics in the Age of Gladstone and Rosebery* (1972), pp. 113–16; for Harcourt's interpretation see Joseph Chamberlain, *A Political Memoir*, edited C.H.D. Howard (1953), p. 175–6.

[33]A. Hardinge, *The Life of the Fourth Earl of Carnarvon* (3 vols. 1925), vol. 3, pp. 179, 191–217, 251–61. Hansard, CCXCIX, 1064–1150.

[34]*A Political Memoir*, pp. 185–8.

[35]*Gladstone, Granville 1876–86*, vol. 2, p. 393.

[36]Hammond, p. 355.

[37]*A Political Memoir*, p. 208; correspondence on his resignation, pp. 193–9; meeting of 31 May, pp. 224–5; *Red Earl*, vol. 2, p. 120.

[38]*Gladstone, Granville 1876–86*, vol. 2, p. 414; see also pp. 418, 423.

[39]*Red Earl*, vol. 2, pp. 93, 107–9.

[40]Hammond, p. 685.

[41]N.E. Johnson (ed.), *The Diary of Gathorne Hardy* (1981), p. 728.

[42]Hamer, p. 214.

[43]Ibid., p. 218.

[44]Lord Crewe, *Lord Rosebery* (1931), vol. 1, p. 347.

[45]Add. MS 44347 *passim*.

[46]R.R. James, *Rosebery* (1963), p. 240.

[47]Ibid., p. 254.

[48]Ibid., p. 265.

[49]Ibid., p. 275; p. 286 for alteration of Portal's draft.

[50]Morley, vol. 3, pp. 498–503.

[51]*Red Earl*, vol. 2, p. 266; H.H. Asquith, *Fifty Years of Parliament* (1926), vol. 1, p. 217.

[52]Both quotations are from Mary Drew, (daughter), *Catherine Gladstone* (1919), p. 287.

[53]Morley, vol. 3, p. 529, quoting Salisbury's speech in the House of Lords.

A Note on Sources

The mass of Gladstone papers is preserved in bound volumes in the British Library. The rest (mostly family, but some political and other letters) is preserved in St Deiniol's Library at Hawarden. His diaries are kept in Lambeth Palace Library. I have used the published edition of the diaries which has now reached 1880: M.R.D. Foot and H.C.G. Matthew (eds.) *The Gladstone Diaries* (nine vols., Clarendon, 1968–86), see p. 119. I am grateful to Messrs Longman for permission to use material and, where necessary, to reproduce the wording of my reviews of successive volumes in the *English Historical Review*, 1970, 1976, 1979 and 1987. My debt to Colin Matthew's introductions to the successive volumes is very large. Agatha Ramm, *The Political Correspondence of Mr Gladstone and Lord Granville* (four vols., Royal Historical Society, 1952, Clarendon, 1962) published material from the Granville papers in the Public Record Office as well as from the Gladstone papers in the British Library. Colonial Office and Foreign Office correspondence, Hansard's *Parliamentary Debates* and *Parliamentary Papers* (Bills, Reports, Accounts and Papers) were used in annotating this work and have been referred to again for the present book. Books and articles published by Gladstone himself are listed in Patricia M. Long, *A Bibliography of Gladstone Publications at Saint Deiniol's Library* (Hawarden, undated). A full account of books and articles about Gladstone is to be found under 'Further Reading' in H.C.G. Matthew, *Gladstone, 1809–1874* (Clarendon, 1986). I have attempted to use the groundwork provided by the writers he lists and to relate it to my own research. This is to be found, in addition to the *Gladstone-Granville Correspondence*, in 'The Planting of Italian Power in the Red Sea', *English Historical Review*, 1944; 'Great Britain and

France in Egypt' Prosser Gifford and Roger Louis (eds.), *France and Britain in Africa* (Yale, 1971); 'The Parliamentary Context of Cabinet Government, 1868–74', *English Historical Review*, 1984; 'Gladstone's Religion', *Historical Journal*, 1985; *'Gladstone as Man of Letters'*, printed by Somerville College, Oxford in 1981. The first two titles use Foreign Office files, the second Quai d'Orsay files and both comment on Gladstone and foreign policy. Of published papers of Gladstone's colleagues, E. Drus (ed.), *A Journal of Events during the Gladstone Ministry, 1868–74 by John First Earl of Kimberley* (Royal Historical Society, Camden Series 1958), Peter Gordon (ed.), *The Red Earl. The Papers of the Fifth Earl Spencer* (Northamptonshire Record Society, 1981, 1986) and C.H.D. Howard (ed.), *Joseph Chamberlain. A Political Memoir* (Batchworth, 1953) have been especially useful. References to further sources will be found in the notes to each chapter.

Twelve Books Selected for Further Reading

S.G. Checkland, *The Gladstones. A Family Biography 1764–1851* Cambridge University Press, 1971)

D.A. Hamer, *Liberal Politics in the Age of Gladstone and Rosebery* (Clarendon, 1972)

J.L. Hammond, *Gladstone and the Irish Nation* (Longman, 1938, reprinted with an introduction by M.R.D. Foot, Frank Cass, 1964)

J.L. Hammond and M.R.D. Foot, *Gladstone and Liberalism* (Hutchinson, 1952)

T.A. Jenkins, *Gladstone, Whiggery and the Liberal Party, 1874–1886* (Clarendon, 1988)

H.C.G. Matthew, *Gladstone 1809–1874* (Clarendon, 1986)

John Morley, *Life of Gladstone* (three vols., Macmillan, 1903)

J.P. Parry, *Democracy and Religion. Gladstone and the Liberal Party 1867–1875* (Cambridge University Press, 1986)

Richard Shannon, *Gladstone* (vol. 1., Hamish Hamilton 1982, vol. 2 still to come)

F.B. Smith, *The Making of the Second Reform Bill* (Cambridge University Press, 1966)

E.D. Steele, *Irish Land and British Politics* (Cambridge University Press, 1974)

J.R. Vincent, *The Formation of the British Liberal Party, 1857–68* (Constable, 1966, reprinted with a new introduction Harvester, 1976)

The Author

Formerly Fellow and Tutor in Modern History at Somerville College, Oxford, Dr. Agatha Ramm is now Fellow Emeritus of Somerville College. She has been a Fellow of the Royal Historical Society since 1953 and in 1976 she was granted a D.Litt. by Oxford University. Her other publications include: *The Political Correspondence of Mr. Gladstone and Lord Granville* (4 vols., 1952 and 1962), *Germany 1789–1919* (1967), *Sir Robert Morier 1876–1893, Envoy and Ambassador* (1973) and *Europe in the Nineteenth and Twentieth Centuries* (1984).

The General Editor

Professor Kenneth O. Morgan F.B.A., D.Litt., is Principal of University College of Wales, Aberystwyth, and was formerly Fellow and Praelector of The Queen's College, Oxford. Born in Middlesex of north Cardiganshire and Merionethshire origins, he is an eminent historian and prolific author. He has written extensively and authoritatively on Radical movements in nineteenth-century and early twentieth-century Britain; his titles include *Wales in British Politics 1868–1922* (1963), *Keir Hardie* (1975), *Consensus and Disunity* (1979), *Rebirth of a Nation: Wales 1880–1980* (1981) and *Labour in Power 1945–1951* (1984). He has been editor of *The Welsh History Review* since 1965 and was elected Fellow of the British Academy in 1983.